Interpreting Historical Sequences Using Economic Models

Paul Hallwood

Interpreting Historical Sequences Using Economic Models

War, Secession and Tranquility

palgrave
macmillan

Paul Hallwood
Department of Economics
University of Connecticut
Storrs, CT, USA

ISBN 978-3-030-53853-8 ISBN 978-3-030-53854-5 (eBook)
https://doi.org/10.1007/978-3-030-53854-5

This Palgrave Macmillan imprint is published by the registered company Springer Nature Switzerland AG
The registered company address is: Gewerbestrasse 11, 6330 Cham, Switzerland

This book is dedicated to my wife, Barbara, and three children, Sarah, Alexander, and Philip.

Preface

'All is for the best in the best of all possible worlds'.
Voltaire's Dr. Pangloss in *Candide*

There have been over 150 border changes since the end of the First World War and that's only a fraction of history. Watching videos of European border changes since early-Roman times dazzles the eyes, and with the Indian subcontinent too.[1] Each border change has its own history going back decades and even centuries. Different peoples have been involved, speaking their different languages, having their different religions, different DNAs, different standards of living, facing different foes and, if they were lucky, enjoying their different friends. Sometimes border changes resulted from civil war and sometimes from treaty settlements after international wars. Sometimes civil wars ended with a nation not splitting apart. Sometimes a third country came to the aid of a disadvantaged people, but often not. Sometimes a third country came to the aid of an advantaged people to make sure that the disadvantaged people remained disadvantaged. Sometimes peacekeepers stepped in but usually not. And just sometimes tranquility reigned and no conflicts happened at all.

[1] See 'List of national border changes since World War I', Wikipedia. Videos of border changes are available on YouTube.

Sometimes separate countries volunteered to join together as one, and sometimes a single country chose to split itself apart. Sometimes a country facing secessionists tried to buy them off with extra money or allowed them autonomous government. But sometimes, instead, they sent in troops and many died.

All these different strands of history have been written about, filling many bookshelves, and the reading of it is very interesting. What is different about this short book is that it offers a general framework that applies to all cases, or, perhaps, only to most cases. Time will tell of course.

The model developed in this book is an economic model in which the leaderships of two sides are either pitched against each other, or, else they work with each other with no malice to find answers to the questions of why will borders change, why will new countries be created, why will Empires grow, and why will Empires fade? Discussed are two historically relatively stable situations—those of 'empire' where an entrapped people can't leave even if they wanted to, and of tranquility where any sub-nation has the freedom to move on but chooses not to. And there are two transitional phases, one of war and one of non-resisted secession. Altogether twelve historical sequences will be discussed.

The economic modeling approach used is that of standard economics, the neoclassical approach, in which individuals attempt to maximize their own welfare—as they define their own welfare, but subject to whatever constraints they may face. The constraint may be an opposing belligerent force, but it could also be that a sub-nation of people decide they can't be any better than with the tranquility they now enjoy.

Lyme, CT, USA
October 2020

Paul Hallwood

Contents

List of Figures

Chapter 2

Chapter 3

Chapter 4

Chapter 5

Chapter 6

Chapter 8

List of Tables

CHAPTER 1

Introduction

Abstract This chapter lays out the key concepts that underpin the analysis in this book including discussion of international law as it relates to secession, the concepts of the optimal size of countries, economic rent and rent seeking contests, the fundamental contribution of neoclassical economics to understanding decision-making, willingness to pay for secession, and 'triggering events'—the events that set off the historical sequences, the main subject matter of this book. The main objective of the book is stated as to deepen the understanding of the causes of historical sequences in both the grouping and ungrouping of countries.

Keywords Colonialism · Conflict · Decision-making · International law · Secession · Triggering events

1 Introduction

Secessions and unifications of peoples in countries are traditionally the stuff of analysis by historians and political scientists, recently though economists have made contributions. Alesina and Spolaore (2003) offer a pioneering economic analysis modeling the optimal size of nations. They do not however offer an explicit analysis of national expansion or contraction in historical time, implying only that an optimum will be reached.

P. Hallwood, *Interpreting Historical Sequences Using Economic Models*,
https://doi.org/10.1007/978-3-030-53854-5_1

They do recognize, however, that 'the actual dynamics of border formation are complex, and may include several interactions of variables and effects that are difficult or even impossible to capture in simplified equilibrium relationships' (p. 9). This book discusses the crucial 'interaction' variables that condition the process of state-based secessions and formations by introducing a broader and more explicit model than heretofore. It is also worth noting that Blattman and Miguel (2010) point out that existing models of civil war are not well supported empirically. This could be because these models do not control for all of the relevant variables, twelve of which being identified in this book, and a change in any one of them could lead to the outbreak of war, or, if war is already going on, to its cessation. As we shall see, these same variables are relevant to both civil and international wars and, as will be shown, they are the drivers of war, secession, and tranquility—the 'absence of war'.

The rational choice model developed here—which is new to the literature on state formation—is paired with many actual cases. This book is not just about theory, and nor is it only about history because theory, to be relevant, needs application and the telling of the story of a history needs a theoretical basis. In other words, this book tells historical 'stories' that have precise theoretical underpinnings. These 'stories' are about state-building and state-fracturing, driven mainly by internal events. As Table 1 records, since the end of World War II wars internal to states far outnumber wars between states, and this is why most attention will be paid to internal wars. Even so, a whole chapter using the same economic

Table 1 Ongoing conflicts: annual average per decade

	Intrastate	*Internationalized*	*Extrastate*	*Interstate*
1940s[a]	10	0[b]	5	2
1950s	9	0[c]	5	1
1960s	16	3	3	2
1970s	24	4	1[d]	3
1980s	34	5	0	3
1990s	39	4	0	1
2000s	29	5	0	1
2010s[e]	30	12	0	1

Source Pettersson et al. (2019)
Notes [a]After 1945; [b]Two ongoing in 1946, none in the rest of the 1940s; [c]Three in the decade as a whole; [d]The last extrastate conflict ended in 1975; [e]To and including 2018

modeling approach as used in the rest of this book is devoted to a discussion of international wars.

The number and pattern of independent states has changed markedly over the last 200 years. According to a data set on the birth and death of states recorded in the International Systems Dataset (ISD), there are slightly fewer independent countries today than there were in 1816. Care is needed in defining what a state is especially in the early years because legally recognized international borders were not always defined. A 'state', according to Butcher and Griffiths (2020), is a geographic entity with a government that has internal control over its territory as well as formal control over its' international relations.

The nineteenth century saw a sharp decline in the number of independent countries largely due to the spread of colonialism through Africa and Asia. According to the ISD, there were 211 independent states in 1816 falling to 58 prior to World War I. Thereafter the number of independent states, as measured by UN membership, rose to 193 in 2020. In both the pre- and post-World War I periods, state births and deaths occurred with, the earlier period, deaths being more frequent than births, while in the later period the opposite is true.

There were 51 United Nations members at inception in 1945, with only 29 of them being outside of the Western Hemisphere. There are several reasons for this growth in membership—the end of colonialism in the Asian subcontinent led to the early membership of India and Pakistan; in Africa south of the Sahara, 32 African countries joined in the eleven years up to 1968, with several more after that date as the colonial powers continued their withdrawals from that continent. In a few cases, the end of colonialism was preceded by serious violence but in many cases not at all. Indeed, Emerson (1965) commented on how little violence was involved at the end of colonialism. By contrast, the violent breakup of Yugoslavia led to the admission to the United Nations of three new independent states in 1992, with several more added to 2006—see Chapter 3. Sometimes two new UN members were created when an existing member split apart, as when Montenegro and Serbia were admitted as separate independent states in 2006 having had a single membership for some years prior to that; similarly, with Egypt and Syria that had formed the United Arab Republic during 1958–1961, and with Malaysia and Singapore in 1965. An example in the reverse direction is the combining into a single member of Yemen and the People's Democratic Republic of Yemen in 1990. In the Persian Gulf area, several states gained independence

Table 2 State-based armed conflict by type in 2018

Type of conflict	*Definition*	*Number active in 2018*
Intrastate conflicts	Conflict between a government and an internal group	32
Internationalized conflicts	Internal conflict involving foreign troops on the ground	18
Extrastate conflicts	Between a government and a non-state group outside of its territory	0
Interstate conflicts	International wars	2

Source Pettersson et al. (2019)

beginning in the 1950s a process running to 1971 with the ending of British Protectorate status. The first South East Asian state to join the UN was Thailand (then called Siam) in 1946, Burma in 1948, Malaysia in 1957, and many more thereafter.

The split or attempted split of a state can be a violent process as is indicated in Table 2 that records the incidence of ongoing state-based armed conflicts in 2018. Intrastate conflicts are between a government and an internal armed group—in 2018, there were 32 of these ongoing. Internationalized conflicts are also internal but with foreign troops participating—Afghanistan and Syria are prominent examples. Extra-state conflicts are between a government and a non-state group outside of its territory. These were mainly involved with the ending of colonialism; the last recorded case was in 1975. Finally, there are interstate conflicts—i.e., international wars; in 2018, there were just two of these—between Israel and Iran and India and Pakistan; and in both cases, the violence was quite limited.

Table 1 shows the record of these four types of conflict by decade between 1946 and 2018. It is apparent that intrastate conflicts have predominated throughout this 72-year period and that internationalized conflicts have become more frequent in recent decades.

2 The Neoclassical Approach

The basic assumption made in this book is that national- and sub-national level decision-makers attempt to maximize an objective value function under a cost constraint. This assumption is very familiar to economists.

The advantage is its generality. Rather than having to develop different theories for disparate geographical and historical events, say, the causes of the end of British rule in India and the causes of the US annexation of Texas, a general theory is offered.

A change in national borders is seen as being a 'transaction' in international law. As such, changes in borders are subject to transaction costs. In the models discussed in the following chapters, there are two types of transaction cost—'*dispute cost*', incurred by an entity—such as a region of a larger union, that pursues independence; and '*persuasion cost*', that is incurred by the larger entity—say, a unified state such as the UK trying to retain Scotland's membership in it, or, an 'empire', such as was the Soviet Union that until its demise aimed at persuading 'sub-regions', say, Hungary in 1956, not to leave its Union.

It is argued that changes in borders depend on the interaction of the *net* benefits of potential secession for a secessionist minded region and the *net* benefit of the larger union of retaining the region as a part of itself. These region-to-union interactions are shown in Chapters 2 and 3 to define four broad historical situations: Tranquility of a region(s) within a union; empire, in which the union would not let a sub-region seceded even if it wanted to; war of secession; and non-resisted secession. This analysis is extended in Chapter 5 to a discussion of the basic politico-economic forces leading to international wars over territory and, in the opposite direction, to the creation of international unions of still largely independent states, such as the European Union *circa* 2020.

The following analysis, based on rational choice theory prominent in economics, uncovers twelve common historical patterns that relate to the stability, expansion, and collapse of states and unions. Examples of each are discussed.

The term 'region' has already been used several times, and in a geographic sense, the meaning is clear. However, quite often, the type of 'region' referred to is typically composed of a sub-nation of people. An example is the people of Kosovo, being mainly of Albanian origin, seeing themselves as being different to the Serbs of Serbia and this was a reason why they wanted to, and did, seceded from that country in 2008. Also, the people of a disadvantaged sub-nation may press not to secede from a union but to gain greater representation in it. This too can lead to civil war. This later proposition is supported by the empirical work of Bang and Mitra (2017) who in their statistical work find that a pre-conflict expected increase in the level of democracy post-conflict significantly increases the probability of a conflict occurring—that is, people fight for greater political representation.

3 International Law and Secession

International public law (IPL) governs legal relationships between states. It is created by states and international organizations composed of states. The United Nations is one such international organization that is heavily involved in interstate politics as well as in peacekeeping operations—as is discussed in Chapter 6. There are two types of international public law, customary and treaty (international private law is quite separate). Customary international law is 'standard practice' between states and bears no signatures. Treaty law is written down and has to be signed and ratified. The United Nations was formed under treaty law.

Legal scholars ask the question 'where does international public law come from'? There are three theories: (1) *Jus Cogens* is 'compelling law' based on universal principles that have to be complied with and being 'universal' it is clear what laws should be complied with. However, this theory of IPL is widely rejected by legal scholars. (2) The positivist theory of utility maximization: states comply with IPLs when it is in their interests to do so, otherwise they do not. This has the important implication that IPL does not change state behavior (see Goldsmith and Posner 1999, 2005). In the case of customary international law, a state can simply choose not to 'join in'; and with treaty law, it can choose not to sign it, or, if it does, to take 'reservations' so not having to abide by possibly crucial clauses. (3) The moral obligation theory, in which IPL is based on shared social norms such as human rights. Because moral obligations may change so will utility payoffs possibly leading to new international law. The argument can be made therefore that the moral obligation and utility maximization sources of IPL blend into one another. Constant repetition in the news media of 'advanced countries' of human rights abuses in states suffering civil wars may change moral precepts leading them to support the international provision of, say, peacemaking or peacekeeping forces. If enough states change in this way, new international customary law is created.[1]

[1] See Busquets (2018) for an argument that moral justifications should play a role in the issue of secession and the creation of new states.

IPL has no overriding policing power, which is very different to laws within sovereign states where people are compelled to comply on pain of punishment. IPL therefore is weaker than national law as sovereign states can refuse to abide by laws they don't like. Why obey IPL when there are no enforcement mechanisms? The disciplining device is 'reputation for compliance'—reputation for complying with international law is valuable because it can stimulate reciprocity.

If IPL is simply based on utility maximization, it does not affect state behavior—'they would do it anyway'. Brunnee and Troope (2011), however, argue that the making of international public law is really based on shared social norms and that these norms are not exogenous to the social, economic, and security interests of states. As social norms develop over time, they will in turn influence the development of IPL.

International law has for about a century recognized a right to self-determination by colonial peoples, but it does not recognize a right to secession. The United Nations Charter refers to rights of self-determination for sub-nations of people, but it does not expressly recognize a general right of secession. Article 55 of the UN Charter states that 'With a view to the creation of conditions of stability and well-being which are necessary for peaceful and friendly relations among nations based on respect for the principle of equal rights and self-determination of peoples, the United Nations shall promote ... universal respect for, and observance of, human rights and fundamental freedoms for all without distinction as to race, sex, language, or religion'. The view of legal scholars though is that this is not enough to establish a right to secession in international law (see, for example, Eastwood 1993; Walter and Ungern-Sternberg 2014).

However, 'there is authority supporting the proposition that a new rule of customary international law can be established within a relatively short period of time so long as there is extensive and uniform state practice evincing general recognition of such a rule' (Eastwood 1993, p. 301). In other words, international law has the potential to change quite quickly, but in the meantime there is no right to secession.

4 Economic Rent and Rent Seeking

Economic rent is a surplus income or reward above supply price. With land, supply price is zero because it exists whether or not it is used. The amount of economic rent therefore depends on the demand for the use of that land, and an upward shift in the demand for it raises the economic rent enjoyed by its owner. This is a standard view of 'economic rent' because it is well established that economic rent generated by an area of land rises when it is moved to more productive uses, say, from farmland to urban land.[2]

What is different in this book is that economic rent increases not because of a change in user within a sovereign country but because of a change in sovereignty over it. If this was not expected to be true, the costs of secession would not be incurred in the first place.

Let us be clear about the nature of the concept of 'economic rent' as the concept is used here. Increases in economic rent are measured by a prospective sovereign most likely in both pecuniary and non-pecuniary terms. Examples of the former are capturing a larger share of taxes levied on a natural resource located on a new sovereign's territory (e.g., as is desired by the Scottish Nationalists of oil tax revenues generated on Scotland's territory—see Chapter 8), and retaining pecuniary earnings that would otherwise be lost (e.g., the profits from slavery in the event of the Confederacy losing the American civil war—see Chapter 7).

Importantly, non-pecuniary benefits can also be generated through changes in sovereignty over an area of land—such as a sub-nation living on it being able to practice its own religion without interference by a larger sovereign power (hence the long-running religious wars in the Middle East and North Africa), or, a sub-nation wanting to make its own laws to provide the public goods it prefers without having to follow the laws of the larger sovereign of which it was once part. These non-pecuniary benefits of sovereignty are referred to in later chapters as the benefits of 'being alone together', and they are measured in pecuniary terms as the 'willingness to pay' for them—the latter being a basic concept in neoclassical economics. An example of how willingness to pay may be measured is discussed in Chapter 7. While the foregoing refers to how the economic analysis developed in this book can be applied at the state level, Chapter 5 is devoted to applying the modeling to a discussion of international sequencing with several examples are discussed.

The concept of *'rent seeking'* is central to the economic analysis in this book—the peoples of both regions of states and states are assumed to be driven to maximize economic rent subject to the costs of doing so. The

[2] The concept of economic rent was originally developed by David Ricardo (1819).

rent seeking literature derives from Tullock (1967) where rational choice models are used to examine the idea that in the pursuit of economic rents, rational agents will spend up to the value of those rents.[3] The classic example of rent dissipation is that expected monopoly profits will be wasted in the pursuit of establishing a monopoly, say, by spending on the manipulation of political processes. Rent seeking is then at the intersection of economics and politics.

As mentioned above, in this book the term 'economic rent' is applied not only to economic gains but also to a *willingness to pay* for political, cultural, or religious benefits. For example, a group of people may wish to practice their cultural or religious preferences unencumbered by societal rules set down by a dominant but different political group in their society. If the willingness to pay for these benefits is great enough, the 'out group' may choose to fight to gain new rights either through secession from the state of which they are a part, or, to gain enhanced powers in that state so as to have greater influence over the setting of the rules that govern cultural or religious rights.

Also, relevant is the development within the rent seeking literature of the concept of *'rent seeking contests'* whereby different groups of actors compete for economic rents. Examples of these contests are political campaigns aimed at controlling a state and civil war can also be seen as a rent seeking contest (see Hirshleifer 1989; Nizan 1994).

Each player, or a group of players, has a 'contest success function' that combines the monetary, or, utility value of winning a contest with the probability of doing so (see Skaperdas 1996). In a contest, a player's probability of winning depends on the 'effort' invested in the contest by the opposing players. In this book, 'effort' is measured by dispute cost incurred by a potential secessionist group, and persuasion costs incurred by the central power. Probabilities of success are interactive—the greater the spending on 'effort' the higher is the probability of a given desired outcome. It may be noted though that it is possible that investments made in raising probabilities of success by one or both players will cause the total investment in rent seeking to add up to more than the value of the economic rent being pursued. As the subjective probabilities of winning a contest are important, they are used in several chapters of this book.

[3]The term 'rent seeking' was in fact introduced by Krueger (1974).

In Chapter 7, the American civil war, 1861–1865, is examined as an example of rent seeking. The question studied is whether protection of profits earned through slavery was enough to provoke the Confederacy's secession from the Union, or, whether 'states rights' were the motiving force. The main conclusion drawn from the quantitative analysis in Chapter 7 is that both factors played a role. A novel contribution of Chapter 7 is that it offers a method for calculating the *willingness to pay* for secession, which is an estimate of the degree of 'grievance' that can provoke a civil war. Grievance is separate from the more easily measured 'greed' motive—such as gaining control over the flow of profits derived from a valuable resource.[4]

Also important in the economic analysis of conflict is the issue of how agents balance expected future incomes or other benefits against the present costs of a conflict should a conflict be engaged in. This is a matter of time preference which is distilled into the concept of choice of discount rate. High time preference means that any expected future benefits deriving from a successful outcome will be discounted at a high rate which, in turn, can mean that they are not worth the present cost of obtaining them. Low time preference—equivalent to 'patience'—means that the present value of future incomes may be large and might then outweigh the present costs of fighting for those gains.

People looking to the long term, even with small expected annual gains, may choose to press for secession if they have patience. Sub-nation groups that are motived by common ethnic or religious identities are likely to fall into this category. Alternatively, there is what might be called 'the diamonds complex' whereby a secessionist group getting control of a valuable resource seeks and reaps immediate gains (see Lujala et al. 2005).[5] Here, benefits in the more distant future are discounted at higher rates because it is immediate benefits that are sort after. Moreover, 'lootable' diamonds—those easy to extract from the earth as opposed to deposits in deep mines that are non-lootable—can be used to finance secessionist movements, thereby increasing the supply of arms and probability of secession.

[4] On greed and grievance, see Collier and Hoeffler (2000).

[5] Lujala et al. (2005) also find in their statistical analysis that discovery of valuable easily marketed mineral deposits is associated with promoting ethnic tensions.

Basuchoudhary and Razzolini (2018) point out that when a secessionist movement is made up of more than one group, if it is not to splinter, the respective groups need to have similar discount rates. For example, if one group became more impatient, raising its discount rate and lowering the present value of expected future benefits of secession, it may splinter from the other group(s) or even cease hostilities.

Given that rent seeking contests are wasteful, political institutions have been developed to limit them. An example of a rent seeking contest-limiting institution is fiscal autonomy. By devolving power downward from central government to a subcentral government in a region, disputes over rent-sharing may be defused. An example is discussed in Chapter 8 which is on the devolution of many spending and taxing powers to the newly created (in 1999) Scottish Parliament in Edinburgh from central government in London.

Contests may also involve negative externalities which are the case with a civil war where neighboring countries suffer negative spillovers—being close to a civil war zone may damage a country's economy by reducing its rates of investment or economic growth, and fighting may spill across borders. Or, the externality may be an offense against, cultural, moral, or religious sensibilities—people feel concerned about the mayhem of war even if it is somebody else's war. To contain these sorts of externalities peacekeeping missions are invested in by outside players, as is the case with UN and NATO peacekeeping missions and those of several other international institutions such as those led by the African Union. Peacekeeping is then aimed at modifying the progression of historical sequences and it is examined in Chapter 6. The main aim of peacekeeping is to increase the probability that a war will not reignite which, depending on circumstances, means increasing the chances that a secession will happen, or, if a civil war was over control of a state, that new power-sharing institutions will be developed.

5 Historical Sequences and Triggering Events

What though causes civil war? Paldam (2020) identifies 'triggering events' as causing political regime changes in a set of 170 countries over the period 1960–2015.[6] Triggering events are 'proximate causes' with some degree of exogeneity; further back in time are 'ultimate' causes.

Triggering events are categorized into four groups: (i) 'domestic political'—such as demonstrations or riots, rulers taking steps toward or away from democracy, collapse of policy, violent coups, and civil wars; (ii) 'domestic economic'—including negative economic growth, and high inflation; (iii) 'external political'—including the collapse of empire or external wars won or lost; and (iv) 'external economic'.

Paldam (2020) identifies 262 triggering events of which 215 are domestic political, 40 external political, 11 domestic economic, and none external economic.[7] External political triggering events peaked during 1989–1993 corresponding to the collapse of communism in Europe.

Prior to regime change in a country, it is usual for numerous significant events to occur. In Paldam's data set, there were on average 2.5 such events per subsequent regime change. Some of these events are classified as 'background' events. Knowing which were background and which were triggering events is a matter of judgment by informed journalists-on-the-ground and, later, by historians and political scientists. When an event causes only regime 'adjustment', it is defined as a background event. Ekelund and Thornton (2020) discuss 200 years of background events leading to the French Revolution in 1789. These were the rent seeking and rent protecting strategies of the clergy and nobility through which they benefited by shifting taxation on to the bourgeoisie and preventing upward mobility of the rest of the population. The triggering event they see as the philosophical revolution known as the Enlightenment that challenged existing institutions and promoted the idea of individualism.

Thus, it is acknowledged that a triggering event immediately preceding a regime change itself will depend on prior historical prior event(s) that could have happened decades prior—there are historical domino effects.

[6] The identification is based on the polity index and articles appearing at the time in The Economist. There is strong agreement on identification between these two sources.

[7] These sum to more than 262 because some triggering events fall into more than one category.

In terms of evolutionary game theory, there is an 'evolution' of events leading up to a regime change. However, knowing how a triggering event at the end of a series of background events depends on earlier events most probably requires book-length analysis on a case-by-case basis. This is why the concise analysis offered in this book abstracts from background events, concentrating instead on triggering events.

6 Conclusions

The record of intrastate and interstate conflicts shows that on a historical scale both are frequent events. This book asks why this is so, and this chapter has outlined the key concepts that are used to answer the important questions about these historical sequences. These include war costs, economic rent and rent seeking contests, the fundamental contribution of neoclassical economics to understanding decision-making by involved parties, the concept of willingness to pay for secession, and 'triggering events'—events that set off historical sequences.

References

Alesina and Spolaore. (2003). *The Size of Nations*. Cambridge: MIT Press.

Bang, J. T., & Mitra, A. (2017). Institutions, Information, and Commitment; The Role of Democracy in Conflict. *Journal of Peace Economics, 28*(2), 165–187.

Basuchoudhary, A., & Razzolini, L. (2018). The Evolution of Revolution: Is Splintering Inevitable? *The Economics of Peace and Security Journal, 13*(1), 43–54.

Blattman, C., & Miguel, E. (2010). Civil War. *Journal of Economic Literature, 48*(1), 3–57.

Brunnee, J., & Troope, S. J. (2011). Interactional International Law: An Introduction. *International Theory, 3*(2), 307–318.

Busquets, P. B. (2018). *Morality and Legality of Secession: A Theory of National Self-Determination*. New York: Palgrave-McMillan.

Butcher, C. R., & Griffiths, R. D. (2020). States and Their International Relations Since 1816: Introducing Version 2 of the International System(s) Dataset (ISD). *International Interactions, 46*(2), 291–308.

Collier, P., & Hoeffler, A. (2000). Greed and Grievance in Civil War. *Policy Research Working Paper 2355*, World Bank.

Eastwood, L. S. (1993). Secession: State Practice and International Law after the Dissolution of the Soviet Union and Yugoslavia. *Duke Journal of Comparative and International Law, 3,* 299–349.

Ekelund, R. B., & Thornton, M. (2020). Rent Seeking as an Evolving Process: The Case of the Ancient Regime. *Public Choice, 182,* 139–155.

Emerson, R. (1965). Colonialism, Political Development, and the UN. *International Organization, 19*(3), 484–503.

Goldsmith, J. L., & Posner, E. A. (1999). A Theory of Customary International Law. *The University of Chicago Law Review, 66*(4, Autumn).

Goldsmith, J. L., & Posner, E. A. (2005). *The Limits of International Law.* Oxford: Oxford University Press.

Hirshleifer, J. (1989). Conflict and Rent-Seeking Success Functions: Ratio vs Difference Models of Relative Success. *Public Choice, 63*(2), 101–112.

Krueger, A. (1974). The Political Economy of the Rent-Seeking Society. *American Economic Review, 64*(3), 291–303.

Lujala, P., Gledistsch, N. P., & Gilmore, E. (2005). A Diamond Curse? *Journal of Conflict Resolution, 49*(4), 538–562.

Nizan, S. (1994). Modelling Rent-Seeking Contests. *European Journal of Political Economy, 10*(1), 41–60.

Paldam, M. (2020). A Study of Triggering Events: When Do Political Regimes Change? *Public Choice, 182,* 181–199.

Pettersson, T., Hogbladh, S., & Oberg, M. (2019). Organized Violence 1989–2018 and Peace Agreements. *Journal of Peace Research, 56*(4), 589–603.

Ricardo, D. (1819). *On the Principles of Political Economy and Taxation.* England: John Murray.

Skaperdas, S. (1996). Contest Success Functions. *Economic Theory, 7,* 283–290.

Tullock, G. (1967). The Welfare Costs of Tariffs, Monopolies, and Theft. *Western Economic Journal, 5*(3), 224–232.

Walter, C., & Ungern-Sternberg, A. (2014). Introduction. In Ungern-Sternberg Walter & K. Abushov (Eds.), *Self-Determination and Secession in International Law.* Oxford: Oxford University Press.

CHAPTER 2

The Economic Model

Abstract An accessible economic model is set out in which to frame historical sequences in intrastate and interstate conflicts. The key determinant of a demand for secession by a sub-nation of people is whether the expected increase in its welfare (economic rents) is greater than the expected costs of making that secession occur. The state of which the sub-nation is a part makes similar calculations, namely, is the expected benefit of retaining the sub-nation as a member of the country worth the expected cost of doing so? Costs may only take the form of financial subsidies to a sub-nation, but they can range all the way up to military expenditures.

Keywords Benefit-cost calculation · Empire · Rational choice · Secession · Sub-nation · Union

1 A Simplified Union

Imagine a 'Union' of two or more regions: it could be a voluntary union of countries such as is the four countries of the United Kingdom or the 50 states of the USA. It could also be an empire where membership of at least one region is not entirely voluntary, the nineteenth- and early-twentieth-century British and French empires are examples, as are the Baltic states in the Soviet Empire. The inhabitants of the different

P. Hallwood, *Interpreting Historical Sequences Using Economic Models*,
https://doi.org/10.1007/978-3-030-53854-5_2

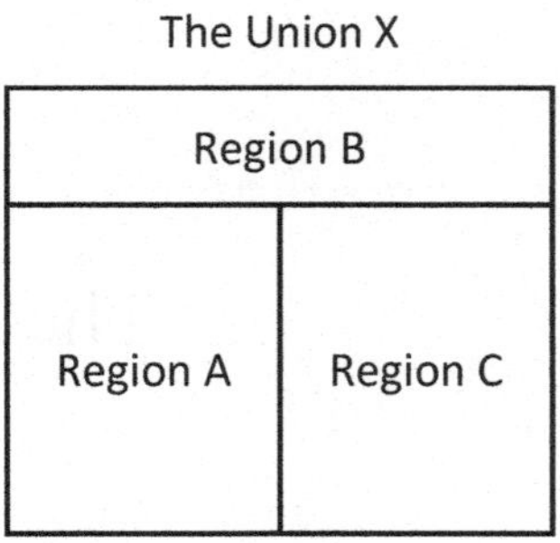

Fig. 1 A Union composed of three regions (*Source* Author's creation)

regions of a Union for some reason may see themselves as being different from one another. The differences might arise from their different histories stemming from many possible sources—different languages, religions, race, social, legal, economic institutions, and cultures. To what extent these different 'glues' are enough to bind a people together in a homogeneous group—a 'sub-nation'—that attempts with or without success to secede from a Union is the subject of many historical studies. Clearly, a common language was not enough to bind the Irish and English together; and while different religions led to the partition of India when the British left, Islamic East Pakistan eventually seceded from the rest of Pakistan which is also Islamic.[1]

In Fig. 1, the Union X is shown as having three regions A, B and C; there could be more of course.

A region will rationally not wish to remain in the Union X if expected benefits from gaining independence exceed the cost of creating a sovereign boundary between itself and what remains of the Union.

What exactly the benefits of sovereignty are thought to be will vary from case to case. The supposed benefits are held in the minds of 'separatists'—meaning those people who identify with a region rather than with the Union as a whole. We define these benefits as the 'economic rent of sovereignty'. As discussed in Chapter 1, the term 'economic rent' indicates a surplus enjoyed by some group or groups, in its original usage, owners of land, which is apposite in the current context and, also discussed in Chapter 1, such a surplus may be in pecuniary and/or

[1] See Khan (2007).

non-pecuniary terms, the latter being measured by 'willingness to pay'—as in standard economic theory. To be clear, the term 'economic rent' is being used in this book as meaning 'benefit' which in the minds of separatist will be measured against the cost of gaining statehood; similarly, with the leaders of a country of which a sub-nation is a part of, they too will compare benefits with costs of retaining or letting go of a portion of its territory. Using rational choice theory to model state behavior is not new as many analyses of treaty formation attest—see, for example, Barrett (2003), Goldsmith and Posner (2005) and Keohane (2005). Extending rational choice theory to sub-nation decision-makers is a logical extension and has been addressed by, for example, Collier and Hoeffler (2000), Collier and Sambanis (2002), and Grossman (1999). In the former paper, sub-nation decision-makers are warlords and their followers expect to gain financially from secession. In that model wider national, societal, cultural, religious, or ethnic grievances are of secondary concern. However, as Marshall and Gurr (2005) and Ballentine and Sherman (2003) show, frequently these factors are motivational. At the present level of abstraction, we don't have to be concerned with which group in a region is the lead decision-maker and exactly what is in the utility function it is aiming to maximize. In Young (2002), the argument is advanced that both economic (or 'material') factors and political factors enter into secessionist's utility functions, but that economic factors predominate in peaceful secessions. Here, we assume only that decision-makers attempt to maximize a utility function subject to cost constraint.

It is assumed that a state's or a region's interests are synonymous with the interests of the respective political leadership (on the generality of this assumption see Goldsmith and Posner 2005). A political leadership may attempt to identify its interests with the interests of the wider citizenry that it weighs in some way. The less democratic a country is the greater, most likely, will be the gap between the interests of the political leadership and those of the rest of the citizens—but even dictatorships have to take account of the interests of the citizens in order to head off insurrection (Alesina and Spolaore 2003).

As mentioned earlier, some recent literature on secession draws a distinction between 'greed' and 'grievance'. The former has secessionists attempting to increase their income or wealth—such as gaining control over a natural resource; the latter ties them to some 'higher' values such as the right to self-determination which has a moral basis. The fact that many secessionist movements have ended in compromise on greater regional autonomy, or, greater representation for a region in national government, suggests that secessionists are not necessarily wedded to achieving moral imperatives; rather, that they are concerned with gaining net benefits out of a struggle. And the latter implies that secessionists perform, perhaps implicitly, benefit-cost calculations. Bartkus (1999) and Bang and Mitra (2017), for example, use a benefit-cost framework in their analyses of secessionist movements.

The analysis of secession proceeds assuming that region B is a potential secessionist and that its dispute is with the Union X. Subregions A and C have a role in the model only in that they identify with the interests of the Union as a whole.

2 Decision-Making in Region B

The 'leaders'—the decision-makers—in a potential secessionist region—region B, have to estimate how much better off they expect region B to be if secession happened. 'How much better off' means that they compare the region's 'welfare level' (something that we are calling 'economic rent') as what it is now, prior to secession, with what they think it will be after secession. This comparison abstracts from whether the decision-makers are thinking only of their own narrow self-interest, or, of the interests of region B's population as a whole. The assumption is that if secession happens, the increased economic rents will occur regardless of whether they are narrowly or widely shared in a newly independent region B. For example, as is discussed in Chapter 7, the slave-owning leadership of the American Confederacy, 1861–1865, would surely have collected most of the economic benefits from retaining the profit-flows derived from the approximately four million slaves. Certainly, a lot of non-slave owners thought that they would have benefited too, which is evidenced by the fact that in the Confederacy state-level majorities voted for secession prior to secession happening in 1861.

To be clear, the leaders in region B will rationally compare the current level of economic rents with what they think they will be should secession occur.[2]

They will also rationally have to weigh the chance, the probability, of secession happening while recognizing that the leaders of the Union may

[2] Basuchoudhary et al. (2020) also develop a rent maximization model of secession.

resist secession. The more likely is resistance by the Union, the lower is the probability of secession. Thus, region B's probability of secession is interactive with the resistance to it put up by the Union; as discussed later, so is the Union's probability of stopping a secession interactive with region's B's 'investment' in secession. These interactions between probabilities are a complicating factor, but it can be cut through by assuming that at any instance in time they can be taken as given. Moreover, it would pay forward-looking decision-makers on both sides to gauge at any moment of time what the counter-responses might be, and to build that information into their instantaneously assessed probabilities of 'victory'.

Also on the benefits side of secession what must also be taken into account in this 'juggling act' of decision-making is how secessionists value the net expected future benefits of secession, if secession were to happen. If they have patience, even future benefits will be valued highly today, but if they are impatient these will have lower present values. These considerations are about the rate at which expected future net benefits are discounted.

One more thing that will also be central in the minds of rational secessionist leaders is 'what will it cost region B in terms of dispute costs'. These may be low if the Union is happy, but probably reluctantly, to wave good-bye—the end of the British Empire is an example of this. Or, secessionist dispute costs could be high if the Union militarily resists secession—the Union side of the American civil war being a good example, as is French resistance to the independence of Vietnam and Russian resistance to the independence of Chechnya.

A more formal statement of region B's maximization problem is laid out in the next section.

3 Region B's Maximization Problem

The expected benefit at a moment in time, t, for region B of breaking away from a Union is shown in Eq. (1) as:

$$E(economic\,rent\,B) = \sum_{t=1}^{T} \left(\frac{(pr_t(\$rent)_t}{(1+r)^t} - \frac{(1-pr)_t \$x_t}{(1+r)^t}\right) \quad (1)$$

where *E(economic rent B)* is the expected present value of economic rent with independence less any economic rent that would have been available had B remained in the Union. *\$rent* is the annual rent that would be earned if sovereignty is won. This value is expressed in monetary terms; *$x* is economic rent if B does not gain sovereignty, so remaining in the Union. pr_t is the subjective probability of gaining sovereignty in any given year $t = 1 \ldots T$; therefore, $(1-pr_t)$ is the probability of not having gained sovereignty in year t; T is the number of years over which secessionists look forward—this could be only to a relatively immediate future or more long term; and r is the decision-makers' rate of time preference.[3]

As mentioned above, the numerical value of the terms in Eq. (1) may change over time. The probability of winning sovereign rights, pr_t, changes with circumstances—for example, if the commitment of the representatives of the Union X to sustaining the Union is thought to have weakened, pr_t may increase. The rate of time preference, r, may change if secession is thought to have become more or less urgent in the minds of decision-makers. And annual economic rents under the different regimes, respectively, $\$rent_t$ and $\$x_t$, may also change. Discovery of a natural resource such as oil or diamonds in region B raises $\$rent_t$ relative $\$x_t$ if that increased rent has to be shared with the Union as a whole—which was the basis in the 1970s of the separatists' cry 'It's Scotland's oil!'.

If region B's secession is not agreed, nationalists there may wish to continue to press for secession. But there is a cost of maintaining a dispute. The expected discounted present value of *dispute cost* is shown in Eq. (2) as:

$$E(dispute\cos t) = \sum_{t=1}^{T} \left(\frac{(1 - pr)_t(\$dispute\cos t)_t}{(1 + r)^t}\right) \tag{2}$$

where $(1-pr)_t$ is again the subjective probability of not having sovereignty in any given year, t, in which case an annual dispute cost is incurred. These costs may be low—just the cost of a negotiating team. But they could be substantial—as when military conflict breaks out.

The *net* advantage to region B of continuing a secessionist dispute is:

$$E(net\ economic\ rent)_B = E(economic\ rent\ B) - E(dispute\ cost) \tag{3}$$

Or,

$$E(NER)_B = (\text{Eq.}1) - (\text{Eq.}2) \tag{4}$$

[3] For a discussion of choice of discount rate in an international relations context, see Streich and Levy (2007).

Whether region B chooses to pursue secession or remains as a part of a larger Union depends, respectively, upon whether $E(NER)_B$ is positive or negative.

The forgoing equations assume that all benefits and costs are internalized to region B. This may not always be the case. An outside power might choose to subsidize region B's dispute costs by, for example, supplying armaments for free or otherwise intervening—as NATO did in Kosovo's secession from Yugoslavia. Similarly, some of the benefits of secession may spillover to third countries, for example, if a third country were to benefit from the breakup of the Union X—a weaker Union X becoming a less formidable foreign policy competitor, as with the decline of any empire.

4 The Union's Side

The government of the Union has essentially the same set of calculations to make leading it to either accept or to reject a secessionist demand from region B. Firstly, it has to assess the *net benefit* to the Union of retaining region B in the Union. This will involve a comparison of what the Union's welfare, its economic rent, would be if region B remained in the Union compared with the presumably lower economic rent if secession happened. Secondly, the Union too will have to assess the probability of retaining B in the Union, something that will depend on numerous things—especially the strength of B's conviction to secede and its willingness to invest in secession, investments that might be just political pressure (e.g., Scotland in the UK) but leading all the way up to paramilitary activities (e.g., secessionists in Northern Ireland). The Union's leaders will also have to assess the strength of its own population's desire to resist secession.

Thirdly, the Union will have to assess its own degree of *patience*. If it is patient—with a low discount rate, it will value relatively highly the expected future benefits of retaining region B in the Union. However, if it discounts those expected future benefits at a high discount rate—meaning that benefits far off in the future are not so important to the Union, the economic return from retaining region B in the Union will seem not to be so large.

Fourthly, the Union will have to consider what here is called its 'persuasion costs'. These are the counterpart of region B's 'dispute costs'. Persuasion costs are the costs of persuading region B to remain in the

Union. These costs might take only the form of, say, subsidizing public expenditure in region B, but they could also run up to expensive levels if military activities have to be invested in, for example, as the British did in attempting to quell the 'Troubles' in Northern Ireland.

5 The Union's Maximization Problem

The government of the Union X has a set of calculations to make. It has to consider the return it gets from retaining region B in the Union in comparison with the cost of persuading B to remain a part of it. At time t, the Union's expected net economic rent from retaining B in the Union is:

$$E(economic\, rentX) = \sum_{t=1}^{T} \left(\frac{(1 - Pr_t)(\$RENT)_t}{(1+i)^t} - \frac{\mathrm{Pr}_t\, \$y_t}{(1+i)^t}\right) \quad (5)$$

where Pr_t is X's subjective probability of B seceding (and may well be different from pr_t which is B's subjective probability of secession). $(\$RENT)_t$ is economic rent enjoyed by the Union with region B remaining in the Union, and $\$y_t$ is the economic rent that it may earn if region B secedes. Finally, i is the Union leadership's rate of time preference. It is reasonable to assume that $(\$RENT)_t$ is greater than $\$y_t$, perhaps substantially so, as with B in the Union, the Union can tax resource rents in region B, while it cannot do so once region B has seceded. And there may be other advantages of keeping region B in the Union such as it being a buffer against unfriendly states.

The Union X incurs a cost of persuading region B to remain within the Union. Persuasion cost could be the extra subsidies given by the Union to region B in an effort to make remaining in the Union favorable for region B. The UK's substantially higher per capita public spending in Scotland following the discovery of North Sea oil in the 1970s is a case in point—see Chapter 8. Also included in persuasion cost is any military expenditures by the Union—such as the stationing troops in region B—as was typical of imperial powers.

Persuasion cost is increased if the Union X comes into conflict with the 'international community' if it tries savagely to resist secession. As Gurr (2000) notes: 'the new liberal wisdom holds that sovereignty can be trumped by humanitarianism and the international cavalry will ride to the rescue of minorities who face genocide' (p. 61). Bosnia and Kosovo in recent history are cases in point. It is also interesting that Rouen (2004) finds that 'an effective state bureaucracy undermines the rebels, but a strong government army does not necessarily enhance the government cause'. An 'effective state bureaucracy' suggests that it operates at low cost to 'undermine' secessionists.

Persuasion cost is:

$$E(persuasion\cos t) = \sum_{t=1}^{T} (\frac{(1 - \mathrm{Pr})_t(\$persuasion\,cost)_t}{(1+i)^t}) \qquad (6)$$

From the Union's point of view, the expected net benefit—the expected net economic rent, $\mathrm{E(NER)_X}$, of region B remaining in the union is:

$$\mathrm{E(NER)_X} = \mathrm{Eq.(5)} - \mathrm{Eq.(6)} \qquad (7)$$

$\mathrm{E(NER)_X}$ is used in this book in the analysis of whether the Union X will agree to secession, by region B. Which it will if $\mathrm{E(NER)_X}$ is negative because keeping region B in the Union is not worth the fight (political or military); secession will occur. Alternatively, if $\mathrm{E(NER)_X}$ is positive, secession will be resisted.

As with region B's costs and benefits, those of the Union X may also be externalized. For example, persuasion costs may be reduced through alliances. Benefits may also be shared with third countries, the US working to keep Latin American countries out of the Soviet orbit most probably allowed other Western countries to have greater volumes of trade with Latin America.

6 Conclusions

This chapter has set out an economic model in which to frame the analysis of historical sequences in both intrastate and interstate conflicts, or, the absence thereof—a condition of tranquility. The key determinant of a demand for secession by a sub-nation of people is whether the expected increase in its welfare is greater than the expected costs of making that secession occur. The benefits of secession are measured in both pecuniary and non-pecuniary terms (the latter as the willingness to pay for them). The state in which a sub-nation resides makes similar calculations—is the expected benefit of retaining the sub-nation as a member of the country worth the expected cost of doing so? Costs may take the form of financial subsidies to a sub-nation, but they can range all the way up to military expenditures. The same 'rent-seeking subject to cost constraints' analysis is also shown to apply to international conflicts.

References

Alesina and Spolaore. (2003). *The Size of Nations*. Cambridge: MIT Press.

Ballentine, K., & Sherman, K. (Eds.). (2003). *The Political Economy of Armed Conflict: Beyond Greed and Grievance*. Boulder: Lynne Rienner Publishers.

Bang, J. T., & Mitra, A. (2017). Institutions, Information, and Commitment; The Role of Democracy in Conflict. *Journal of Peace Economics, 28*(2), 165–187.

Barrett, S. (2003). *Environment and Statecraft: The Strategy of International Treaty Making*. Oxford: Oxford University Press.

Bartkus, V. O. (1999). *The Dynamic of Secession*. Cambridge: Cambridge University Press.

Basuchoudhary, A., Hentz, J. J., & Rhamey, A. P. (2020). *Modeling How Rents Change the Nature of Conflict: An Analytical Narrative of Conflict in Nigeria*. https://www.researchgate.net/publication/338825751_Modeling_How_Rents_Change_the_Nature_of_Conflict_An_Analytical_Narrative_of_Conflict_in_Nigeria.

Collier, P., & Hoeffler, A. (2000). Greed and Grievance in Civil War. *Policy Research Working Paper 2355*, World Bank.

Collier, P., & Sambanis, N. (2002). Understanding Civil War: A New Agenda. *Journal of Conflict Resolution, 46*(1), 3–12.

Goldsmith, J. L., & Posner, E. A. (2005). *The Limits of International Law*. Oxford: Oxford University Press.

Grossman, H. I. (1999). Kleptocracy and Revolution. *Oxford Economic Papers, 51*, 267–283.

Gurr, T. R. (2000, May/June). Ethnic Warfare on the Wane. *Foreign Affairs, 79*(3), 52–64.

Khan, Y. (2007). *The Great Partition: The Making of India and Pakistan*. New Haven: Yale University Press.

Keohane, R. (2005). *After Hegemony: Cooperation and Discord in the World Political Economy*. Princeton: Princeton University Press.

Marshall, M. G., & Gurr, T. R. (2005). *Peace and Conflict*, Chapter 2, The Peace and Conflict Ledger: Country Ratings of Peace-Building Capacity in 2005. *Center for International Development and Conflict Management*, University of Maryland. http://members.aol.com/cspmgm/PC2005.pdf.

Rouen de, J. R. (2004). The Dynamics of Civil War Duration and Outcome. *Journal of Peace Research, 41*(3), 303–320.

Streich, P., & Levy, J. S. (2007). Time Horizons, Discounting and Intertemporal Choice. *Journal of Conflict Resolution, 51*(2), 199–226.

Young, R. (2002). Economic Factors in the Secession Calculus: A Survey, paper presented to the *Conference on Economics of Political Integration and Disintegration*, Catholic University of Louvain, May.

CHAPTER 3

Intrastate Sequencing with Historical Examples

Abstract The underlying economic model set out in Chapter 2 is shown to yield two sets of historically stable equilibria—empire and tranquility—and two transitional equilibria—war of secession and non-resisted secession. Each of the four categories is then populated with examples from recent history. This approach is easily applied to categorize events in any historical period.

Keywords Empire through manipulation · Empire through occupation · Non-resisted secession · Tranquility · Unitary and federal states · War of secession

1 Introduction

The view in this book is that excitement of study of historical sequences is found in how a Union's and potential secessionists payoffs line up against each other. At a given moment in time, there are four possible combinations of payoffs:

1. The net payoff is positive for secessionists and negative for the Union.
2. The net payoff is negative for secessionists but positive for the Union.

P. Hallwood, *Interpreting Historical Sequences Using Economic Models*,
https://doi.org/10.1007/978-3-030-53854-5_3

3. The net payoffs are positive for both sides.
4. The net payoffs are negative for both sides.

In case 1, secessionists will press for secession and as the Union sees no net benefit for itself in resisting, a non-resisted secession will happen. This corresponds with the breakup of the Soviet Empire in Eastern Europe at the end of the 1980s.

In case 2, as potential secessionists see no net benefit at the present time for themselves in trying to force secession and that the Union would resist (or, continue to resist), no secession will occur.

In case 3, as the net benefits are positive for both sides—the secessionists want to seceded and the Union chooses to resist secession a secessionist dispute will begin, or, if it is already underway, it will continue. This could mean paramilitary verses military action, or, it could be much less dramatic with the secessionists continuing to engage in political action in favor of secession, while the Union tries to persuade a secessionist region B to remain in the Union with a series of political and economic favors. The offer of favors corresponds with secessionist minded Scotland being granted them by the rest of the United Kingdom—see Chapter 8.

In case 4, tranquility reigns because region B does not want to secede and the Union would not resist secession should it be asked for. The payoffs of the two sides are shown in Fig. 1. The present value of expected *net* economic rents for region B and the Union X are $E(NER)_B$ and $E(NER)_X$, respectively, Eqs. (4) and (7) in Chapter 2. The payoffs in the lower left corner of each box are those for the Union and in the upper right corner those for region B.

The four boxes in Fig. 1 define four historical phases: a tranquil union ('Tranquility'), a stable empire ('Empire'), a war of secession, and a non-resisted secession.

In the southeast box of Fig. 1, the net reward for pressing for secession is negative for region B, and in any event, the Union X would *not* resist as its persuasion cost of retaining B in the Union is greater than the net benefit of doing so. Both region B and X prefer continuation of their Union. Tranquility reigns. Forms of government found in this box include tranquility in unitary states—a state with a central government with power devolved downward but answerable to it; federal states such as Germany; a commonwealth of largely independent states (as with

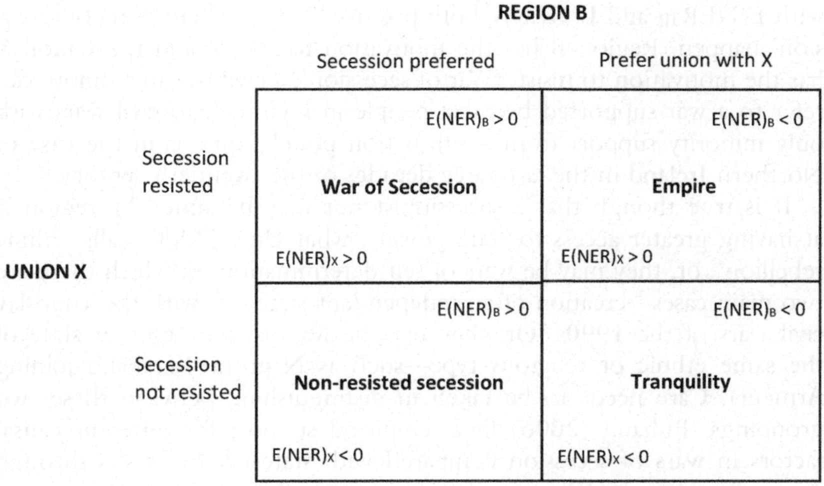

Fig. 1 To secede or not to secede? (*Source* Author's creation)

the British Commonwealth); and in earlier times, intermarriage between kingdoms aimed at sealing alliances.

Secondly, in the northeast box of Fig. 1 expected net economic rent is positive for the Union but negative for region B. This is the case of stable empire. Region B, with negative $E(NER)_B$, does not have sufficient motivation to try to attempt secession, and the Union, with $E(NER)_X > 0$, would resist it if B was to demand it. This is a broad definition of 'empire' as it does not distinguish between 'empire through occupation'—the Roman or French empires, or, 'empire through manipulation'—the US 'empire' of the cold war when secession (e.g., Chile briefly under democratically elected President Allende, 1970–1973) was resisted through subversive activities. Empires though can shade into commonwealths. Thus, assuming that $E(NEB)_B < 0$, the critical value becomes $E(NEB)_X$. Strongly positive values indicate a vigorous system of empire. But reducing the value of $E(NEB)_X$ toward zero—and round about when $E(NEB)_X = 0$, empire may turn into commonwealth.

Thirdly, as we saw in Table 1 in chapter 1, there have been many civil wars since the end of World War II. In a large number of these, conflict was over the division of territory. This is in the northwest box of Fig. 1

with $E(NER)_B$ and $E(NER)_X$ both positive. This is where 'wars of secession' happen. Region B has the motivation to secede and the Union X has the motivation to resist. 'War of secession', a civil war in a union, can refer to a war supported by most people in region B, to civil wars with only minority support from a sub-nation population—as in the case of Northern Ireland in the last three decades of the twentieth century.

It is true though that a secessionist war may be aimed by region B at having greater access to state power—what Gurr (2000) calls 'ethnic rebellion', or, they may be wars of self-determination, of which there are two main cases—creation of an independent state—as with the Yugoslav civil wars of the 1990s. Or, they may be wars to join another state of the same ethnic or religious type—such as Nagorno-Karabakh joining Armenia. Care needs to be taken in distinguishing between these two groupings. Buhaug (2006) finds empirical support for different causal factors in wars of secession compared with state-takeovers—as through a *coup* for example. When a rebel group is strong relative to the state, it may attempt to take over the state; when it is relatively weak and has little chance of taking over the state, the preferred action becomes secession.

Settlement of a civil war may be through region B being granted greater access to power within the existing state, even though the original objective may have been separation. One should not mix up original objective with a compromised outcome. Marshall and Gurr (2005) identify more than a dozen wars of secession being settled by the grant of greater autonomy, rather than separation under international law.

Fourthly, the southwest box shows the case of peaceful—non-resisted—secession: region B desires to secede ($E(NER)_B > 0$) and the Union X has no desire to resist secession as $E(NER)_X < 0$. Secessions in democratic countries are likely to be of this kind, and they are the only type discussed in Alesina and Spolaore (2003). The case of the UK's 'secession' from the European Union in 2020 is a case in point; an imperfect example perhaps—because the UK had not handed over that much sovereignty to the European Union, agreeing only to abide by the rulings of the European Court of Justice and to accept some decision taken by majority vote in the Council of Ministers.

Figure 2 records several cases of secession over the period 1990–2020 that correspond to the four classifications in Fig. 1. In the early years of this period, the Soviet Empire broke up and the USSR dissolved itself. Also, Yugoslavia fell apart with its six constituent regions separating. These two cases, however, are very different: wars of secession did not

REGION B

UNION X	Secession preferred	Prefer union with X
Secession resisted	**War of secession** 1991: South Ossetia (supported by Russia) from Georgia 1994-96 and 1999-2000: Chechen wars of secession resisted by Russia 1992: Nagorno-Karabakh from Azerbaijan; Croatia, Boznia and Herzegovina, Slovenia from Yugoslavia; Abkhazia from Georgia 1993: Eritrea from Ethiopia 1997: Anjouan and Moheli secede to 2002 2011: South Sudan from Sudan 2014: Donetsk and Luhansk regions from Ukraine	**Empire** Chechnya after losing war with Russia
Secession not resisted	**Non-resisted secession** *From* USSR: (1990) Belarus, Abkhazia, Lithuania; (1991) Azerbaijan, Kyrgyzstan, Turkmenistan, Uzbekistan, Armenia, Moldova, Tajikistan, Nagorno-Karbakh, Georgia *From* Yugoslavia: (1991) Macedonia *From* Somalia: (1991) Somaliland *From* South Africa: (1991) Namibia *From* US: (1994) Palau *From* Portugal: (2002) Timor Leste *From* Serbia: (2008) Kosovo	**Tranquility*** 14 British Overseas Territories including Cayman Islands, British Virgin Islands, and Gibraltar 7 French Islands including Reunion, French Polynesia, Martinique, and Guadeloupe

Fig. 2 Some recent historical cases (1990–2020) (*Source* Author's creation) (*Note* *The remaining 14 British Overseas Territories are internally self-governing. However, the UK remains responsible for their defense and foreign policies. Citizenship is of the British Dependent Territories does not give the right to reside in the UK)

materialize when the USSR's Eastern European Empire fell but they did when Yugoslavia broke up. The demise of Yugoslavia was savage with about 140,000 deaths.

2 Collapse of Empires

The economic model offered in this book is now applied to the collapse of two 'empires'—those of the USSR and Yugoslavia.

2.1 USSR and Eastern Europe

The end of the Soviet control in Eastern Europe was laid out in a speech before the United Nations by Russian President Mikhail Gorbachev on December 7, 1988. Two main strands of his speech spelled out a new Soviet philosophy of international relations and planned changes in military deployments in Eastern Europe. Both strands indicated that Russia would cease military intervention in Eastern Europe.

Gorbachev implied that Russia was reducing its investment in persuasion costs, thereby raising the hopes of secession in its East European states. That is, the latter's probabilities of secession increased from, most probably, low levels given the earlier barely externally supported attempted secessions of Hungary in 1956 and Czechoslovakia in 1968. East European dispute costs will also have fallen as Soviet commitment to its empire fell. Moreover, assuming that Soviet expectations of secessions had increased, which surely they must have, its probability weighted benefits (its economic rents) earned in Eastern Europe must also have fallen. The upshot was that the USSR's $E(NER)_X$ turned negative, while in East Europe $E(NER)_B$ turned positive. In other words, the USSR and its East European satellites moved directly from the northeast box in Fig. 1 to the southwest box. The USSR's East European satellites just walked away, there were a series of non-resisted secessions.

In light of the foregoing, it is interesting to consider key parts of Gorbachev's speech referred to above.[1] With respect to international relations, he said:

[1] "Address by Mikhail Gorbachev at the UN General Assembly Session (Excerpts)," December 07, 1988, History and Public Policy Program Digital Archive, CWIHP Archive. http://digitalarchive.wilsoncenter.org/document/116224

> Further world progress is now possible only through the search for a consensus of all mankind, in movement toward a new world order.... It is a question of cooperation that could be more accurately called "co-creation" and "co-development." The formula of development 'at another's expense' is becoming outdated

... which implies that economic rent earned through empire was falling, or, at least, had become tainted and undesirable. Then,

> In these conditions, interference in those internal processes with the aim of altering them according to someone else's prescription would be all the more destructive for the emergence of a peaceful order... It is evident, for example, that force and the threat of force can no longer be, and should not be instruments of foreign policy.

... which implies that increased persuasion costs—the cost of military intervention in Eastern Europe—caused increasing opportunity costs in other international political spheres. Then, Gorbachev said

> Freedom of choice is a universal principle to which there should be no exceptions. We have not come to the conclusion of the immutability of this principle simply through good motives. We have been led to it through impartial analysis of the objective processes of our time. The increasing varieties of social development in different countries are becoming in ever more perceptible feature of these processes. This relates to both the capitalist and socialist systems. The variety of sociopolitical structures which has grown over the last decades from national liberation movements also demonstrates this. This objective fact presupposes ...tolerance, a preparedness to see phenomena that are different as not necessarily bad or hostile, and an ability to learn to live side by side while remaining different and not agreeing with one another on every issue.

...implying that economic rents without an empire, $\$y_t$, were increasing. These were the critical elements of the new Russian foreign policy, and as to the end of Soviet military intervention, Gorbachev said:

> The Soviet Union has made a decision on reducing its armed forces. In the next two years, their numerical strength will be reduced by 500,000 persons, and the volume of conventional arms will also be cut considerably. These reductions will be made on a unilateral basis...

The USSR was dissolved December 25, 1991, becoming the Russian Federation.

2.2 *Yugoslavia's Wars of Secession*

Under President Tito (1953–1980), Yugoslavia and its constituent Republics of Serbia, Croatia, Bosnia and Herzegovina, Macedonia, Slovenia, and Montenegro, could be described as a voluntary Union. Historical, ethnic, and religious differences existed between them but not enough to provoke attempts at secession. This 'voluntary union' view of Yugoslavia under Tito might have been tranquility in the southeast box of Fig. 1 with $E(NER)_B$ negative, but it could also have been that $E(NER)_X$ was positive, something that was never tested. If the latter was the case it would have put the Republics, or some of them, in the northeast box of empire.

The 'test' came following the death of Tito in 1980. Then, a few years later, with the collapse of the USSR and its Eastern European dependent states, the idea arose in the constituent Republics of Yugoslavia except Serbia (the 'central power') and Montenegro that they wanted to seceded from it. However, under President Milosevic, Serbia—which controlled Yugoslavia's army and could have few complaints about its position in Yugoslavia given that its capital was in Serbia and that Serbs dominated the communist party and the armed forces—chose to resist secessions.[2] This moved Yugoslavia to the northwest box of Fig. 1, setting up three wars of secession—with Slovenia, Bosnia and Herzegovina, and Croatia.[3] It must be stressed however that the Croat and Bosnia and Herzegovina wars were complicated by fighting between resident ethnic groups which meant that these wars can also be interpreted as 'civil wars with outside (Yugoslav) support'.

Slovenia and Croatia both declared independence (secession) in June 1991. Slovenia faced a brief 10-day war of secession. Croatia's civil war lasted over 1991 and 1992 when the Yugoslav army ended its direct intervention. However, fighting within Croatia went on until 1995 as a civil

[2] On Serb domination of Yugoslavia, see Malcolm (1994).

[3] The historical and political details of developments in Yugoslavia before, during, and after the wars of secession/civil wars are discussed in great detail by Ramet (2005) in which she assesses more than 130 books and many papers written on these subjects.

war between ethnic Croats and ethnic Serbs. After a referendum on independence, Bosnia and Herzegovina declared independence in early-1992 which led to a very bloody war with about 100,000 deaths.

The Republic of Bosnia-Herzegovina is composed of three ethnic groups—Muslim Bosniaks, Orthodox Christian Serbs, and Catholic Croats. In the referendum on secession, held in early-1992, only the Bosniaks supported secession from Yugoslavia while the Serbs boycotted it. With a majority for secession, Bosnia-Herzegovina declared independence in April of that year. This was a serious miscalculation most probably based on the assumption that the probability of gaining independence, pr_t, had increased and that the central power, the Socialist Federal Republic of Yugoslavia, would accept it (i.e., Pr_t had also increased). However, what this left out of consideration was that the Croats and Serbs in Bosnia-Herzegovina would choose to resist secession; they brought in the Yugoslav army on their side.[4]

3 History Without Costs

It is easy to show that the optimal country size model of Alesina and Spolaore is more restrictive than the more general model offered here because they do not include some critical elements, namely, dispute and persuasion costs and probabilities of certain crucial events happening. In their model, several factors can cause optimal country size to fall, that is for one or more regional secessions to reduce the size of a Union, thereby increasing the number of countries in the world. Important among these size-reducing factors in the Alesina and Spolaore modeling are: (a) a more open world economy; (b) lower transaction costs in international trade and finance; (c) the world becomes more peaceful; (d) decline in the central power of an empire; and (e) rise of nationalist movements. These size-reducing factors are easily incorporated into our model:

a. Development of a more open world economy, which is in fact the case since the end of World War II, tends to raise the value of $E(NER)_B$ by raising $(\$rent)_t$ because more open world trade raises region B's gains from trading with the rest of the world. This is a

[4] See Burg and Shoup (1999). A different view is the war in Bosnia-Herzegovina was really an internal three sided civil war; however, this leaves out of consideration the critical role played by the Yugoslav army.

simple 'gains from trade' argument. Put differently, the value as a public good of an open internal market will decline when international markets are open. It is also likely that the leaders of region B would come to think that the probability of independence would rise, i.e., pr_t increases, as it may well reason that the Union X itself can reap larger gains from international trade, rather than restricting itself to internal trade with region B. Recalculations will also occur in the Union X tending to reduce the value of $E(NER)_X$. The probability of region B leaving, Pr_t, will rise if X realizes that B will push harder for secession (due to the increase in gains from international trade relative to internal trade); and X's 'persuasion costs', $\$(\text{persuasion cost})_t$, are therefore like to rise as B can be expected to press harder for secession.

b. Lower transaction costs in international trade and finance—such as promoted by the Internet. This is similar in its effect point (a) as the openness of the world economy is increased.
c. The world becomes more peaceful. There are several reasons as to why this may occur—a hegemon supplies it, a world body such as UN helps to supply it, or, it is supplied regionally, for example, by the European Union. On this point, Alesina and Spolaore (2003) argue that an unpeaceful world favors large unions as regions huddle together for protection. Peace breaking out therefore tends to reduce the required size of unions. In our model, the effect of a more peaceful world is to raise the value of $E(NER)_B$ as pr_t increases (region B thinks that as X no longer needs such a large sized union it will more readily accept secession by region B); $(\$\text{dispute cost})_t$ may also fall for the same reason; and region B's discount rate could increase as it becomes more impatient to secede. Secondly, the value of $E(NER)_X$ is likely to fall as Pr_t rises as X expects region B to want to secede.
d. Decline in the central power of an empire (e.g., collapse of the USSR) has a rather obvious effect on the desire to secede. First, $E(NER)_B$ increases as it becomes more likely that secession will occur—pr_t increases. Moreover, B's dispute costs, $(\$\text{dispute cost})_t$, are likely to fall as it expects less resistance from X. On the side, $E(NER)_X$ is likely to fall because Pr_t rises as X expects region B to press for secession; region B's discount rate may rise if the new rulers of X are seen as being less patient than the deposed 'dictator' (who can be assumed not to be impatient but to want the empire

to live for 'a thousand years'); and the Union's persuasion costs, $(\$\text{persuasion cost})_t$, are also like to rise given that region B has lost its fear of challenging X for independence. The rise in $E(NER)_B$ and fall in $E(NER)_X$ are the presumed reasons for why the replacement of the USSR by the Commonwealth of Independent States failed to maintain the Russian hegemony to the same extend as did the USSR.

e. A rise in nationalism—as with Italy in the nineteenth century. In this case, $E(NER)_B$ increases as pr_t and impatience (measured by the discount rate, r) both increase. Moreover, $E(NER)_X$ decreases as X (imperial Austria-Hungary in this case) realizes that secession is more likely, Pr_t increases, and $(\$\text{persuasion cost})_t$ rises for the same reason.

4 Conclusions

This chapter has categorized the dynamic events that can lead to historical sequences. Both tranquility and empire can be thought of as historical equilibria in the sense that they can persist for a long time. The other two historical stages—wars of secession and of non-resisted secession—are transitional phases that are likely to be of shorter duration than are the other two. Even so, empires do not last forever and nor must tranquility. A more detailed discussion of these drivers of historical sequences is laid out in the next chapter.

References

Alesina and Spolaore. (2003). *The Size of Nations*. Cambridge: MIT Press.

Buhaug, H. (2006). Relative Capability and Rebel Objective in Civil War. *Journal of Peace Research, 43*(6), 691–708.

Burg, S. L., & Shoup, P. S. (1999). *The War in Bosnia-Herzegovina: Ethnic Conflict and International Intervention*. Sharpe: London, M.E.

Gurr, T. R. (2000, May/June). Ethnic Warfare on the Wane. *Foreign Affairs, 79*(3), 52–64.

Malcolm, N. (1994). *Bosnia a Short History*. New York: New York University Press.

Marshall, M. G., & Gurr, T. R. (2005). *Peace and Conflict*, Chapter 2, The Peace and Conflict Ledger: Country Ratings of Peace-Building Capacity in 2005. *Center for International Development and Conflict Management*, University of Maryland. http://members.aol.com/cspmgm/PC2005.pdf.
Ramet, S. P. (2005). *Thinking about Yugoslavia: Scholarly Debates about the Yugoslav Breakup and the Wars in Bosnia and Kosovo.* Cambridge: Cambridge University Press.

CHAPTER 4

Drivers of Historical Sequences

Abstract The forces driving movement between historical equilibria as sets out in Chapter 3 are developed further to illustrate the rich dynamics driving historical sequences. The basics of nine common historical sequences are discussed and examples of each given.

Keywords Dispute costs · Historical drivers · Monroe doctrine · Persuasion costs · Time preference

1 Introduction

The argument in Chapters 2 and 3 is that historical sequences—the movements between empire, war of secession, non-resisted secession, and tranquility—are driven by combinations of expected net economic rents (that is, *net* benefits) and probabilities of winning between a secessionist minded region B and the Union X of which B is a part. There are six drivers of historical sequences lying behind decision-making in region B—which are the terms in Eqs. (1) and (2) in Chapter 2. There also six historical drivers lying behind decision-making on the Union's side; these are the terms in Eqs. (5) and (6) also found in Chapter 2. These twelve drivers are summarized in Table 1. The left-hand column relates to the region B's drivers, and the right-hand column to the Union's calculations.

P. Hallwood, *Interpreting Historical Sequences Using Economic Models*,
https://doi.org/10.1007/978-3-030-53854-5_4

Table 1 Fundamental drivers of historical sequences

Elements in the calculation of Region B's expected net economic rent: $E(NER)_B$	*Elements in the calculation of Union X's expected net economic rent:* $E(NER)_X$
1. $(\$dispute\ cost)_t$: B's cost of disputing sovereignty with the Union as seen at time t	1. $(\$persuasion\ cost)_t$: the Union's cost of persuading B to remain in the Union as seen at time t
2. $(\$rent)_t$: the return to region B with independence as seen at time t	2. $(\$RENT)_t$: X's return having region B remain in the Union as seen at time t
3. pr_t: B's subjective probability of secession as seen at t. Or, $(1-pr)_t$: region B's subjective probability of secession not occurring	3. Pr_t: the Union's subjective probability of region B seceding. Or, $(1-Pr)_t$: union's subjective probability of region B not seceding
4. r: B's rate of time preference	4. i: union's rate of time preference
5. $\$x_t$: economic rent earned by region B if it remains in the Union as viewed at time t	5. $\$y_t$: the future economic rent earned by the Union if region B leaves the union as seen at time t
6. t...T is B's forward looking time scale from the present, year t, to a future year, year T	6. t...T is X's forward looking time scale from the present, year t, to a future year, year T

Source Author's creation

Consideration is now given to some examples of how the historical drivers listed in Table 1 can work out in practice.

2 Dispute Cost and Persuasion Cost

Dispute cost is the opportunity cost of seeking secession from a Union. It can include expenditures on political activities and diplomacy (secessionist's expenditures in third countries) aimed at promoting the legitimacy of and support for a secessionist cause.[1] Secessionists may appeal to principles of 'human rights' and arguments for self-determination to bolster their case. If hostilities break out, dispute cost will include expenditures on weapons, cost of injuries and lost lives, and costs of lost economic output. Blattman and Annan's (2010) empirical evidence on African civil wars suggests that child inductees into secessionist guerrilla movements lose a year of schooling and, combined with injuries, leads to one-third

[1]For example, as reported in various newspapers in early August 2007 the newly elected Scottish Nationalist government made demands on the Westminster government to enhance Scottish representation in the European Union and in British Embassies.

lower lifetime earnings. Also, Collier and Hoeffler (2000) make the argument that dispute costs depend inversely on both a secessionist region's forest cover and how mountainous is its terrain as these are natural defenses against unionist forces.

Dispute cost of secessionist wars may be externalized within the secessionist region B to a non-supportive-of-secession population—examples are plague, starvation, collateral damage, and lost economic opportunities. To the extent that some part of dispute cost is avoided by secessionist fighters can be expected to encourage them to prolong secessionist war if needs be. An objective of the central power in a Union would be as much as possible to internalize dispute costs to the secessionists. This could mean sharply focused military actions against them that touch non-secessionist minded people in region B as little as possible. In Collier and Hoeffler (2000), secessionists are motivated by greed—to take control of oil or other mineral deposits—and may correctly be assumed not to place much weight on the havoc they may cause around them. Secessionists motivated by grievance however are more likely to want to minimize external cost. An example would be Mahatma Gandhi who, in seeking India's secession from the British Empire, promoted non-violent methods of protest. In Chapter 7, on the American civil war, it is shown that both greed and grievance played as motivating forces in the Confederacy.

Dispute costs falling on secessionists may be shared with a third power. In the American Revolution, the secessionists were supported by France who supplied money, arms, soldiers, naval services, and international recognition of independence. Similarly, following the Soviet invasion of Afghanistan in 1979, local resistance to incorporation into the Soviet Empire received outside support from, among others, Pakistan and the USA. Another example of critical outside power support is East Timor that enabled it to secede from Indonesia in 1999 with the backing of UN, Australian, and New Zealand armed forces. However, Hungary's secessionist movement to leave the Soviet Empire in 1956 and Czechoslovakia's in 1968 received only sympathy but no substantive outside support. These countries had already been ceded by the Western powers to the Soviets in 1945.[2] Their revolts against Soviet authority were easily put down. A further illustration of the importance of third party support to secessionist movements was in August 2007 Russia said

[2] At the Yalta Conference.

that it would recognize South Ossetia (with a secessionist movement from Georgia), if the West recognized the independence of Kosovo from Serbia.[3] Finally, dispute cost is a positive function of a Union's investment in persuasion cost. This would be the case if hostilities break out and the level of fighting escalates.

3 Changes in Expected Economic Rents

Many commentators stress that an increase in the expected benefits of independence is a main driving force of secessionist movements (e.g., Lujala et al. 2005; Mansfield and Snyder 2005; Collier and Hoeffler 2000). The latter reference stresses the direct pecuniary benefits of secession that derive from exploiting natural resources. Subjectivity in ethnic rivalry is stressed by Sen (2006).

If identity is nothing more than a selective figment of the imagination as is argued by Sen (2006), one wonders if some causes of historical sequences are similarly caused by psychological misconceptions. In our model, the two variables that pickup on this are changes in economic rent and changes in the subjective probabilities of secession. First, recognize that the definition of economic rent may include both natural resource rent—the excess return on natural resources that has a realizable pecuniary value, and a non-pecuniary value, as when an ethnic group simply puts a value on being together and separates from some other group who they think are different from them. An increase in natural resource rent can lead to a demand for secession—$E(NER)_B$ turning positive. This may be buttressed by an increase in the non-pecuniary value component of economic rent, especially if warlords, or nationalists of whatever stripe, for self-interested reasons, fan the flames of ethnic diversity. Moreover, demands for secession can stem directly from an increase in this non-pecuniary economic rent unaccompanied by natural resource discoveries. This appears to be the case in Chechnya following the fall of the Soviet Union—there were no new natural resource discoveries there, only that its Muslim population wanted to separate itself from the 'others'—"to be alone together". Willingness to pay for non-pecuniary values of secession is discussed in Chapter 7.

[3] *Financial Times*, August 8, 2007, p. 6.

4 Changes in Subjective Probabilities of Secession

As an historical example, irredentism in the nineteenth-century Italian unification under the effective leadership of Garibaldi can be argued to have raised the probability of secession (pr_t) in the Italian States because the initially distant dream of unification had become more likely. At the same time, his successes probably lowered the Austria-Hungarian Empire's probability of victory ($1-\mathrm{Pr_t}$) so that the Italian States could well secede from the empire (see Riall 1994).

It is entirely possible that misconceptions can cause the subjective probabilities of secession to change, so disturbing an historical equilibrium. There are two interesting cases: first, $\mathrm{pr_t}$ and $\mathrm{Pr_t}$ may be *positively correlated*—that is, as region B's subjective probability of secession rises, the Union also increasingly thinks that secession might well happen. Assuming a starting point of tranquility, something might happen to raise pr_t—perhaps a conception forms in region B that the Union will not resist secession should B press the matter. Something like this seems to have happened in the Soviet Empire during the collapse of communism toward the end of the 1980s—see Chapter 3.

Agitation in region B for secession then raises the probability, $\mathrm{Pr_t}$, in the Union that region B will indeed secede. These changes in the subjective probabilities may be sufficient to move an equilibrium from tranquility to non-resisted secession; or, beginning with empire, also to non-resisted secession—as in fact happened with the Soviet Empire.

Secondly, when region B's probability of gaining secession rises the Union X's leaders might think that this is increasingly unlikely, that is $(1-\mathrm{P_r})_\mathrm{t}$ *falls*—pr_t and $\mathrm{Pr_t}$ are negatively correlated. This is the case of 'war as a self-fulfilling prophecy', and it is a further illustration of the indeterminacy of historical equilibriums. An outside power (not B and not X) may in some material way encourage B to seceded from X, raising pr_t; but the Union X, feeling the threat from the outside power, then resolves to keep B in the Union. This resolve may be great enough to reduce $\mathrm{Pr_t}$. If the changes in the two subjective probabilities are great enough, tranquility can turn into war of secession (when the signs of the expected net economic rents both turn positive due to the changes in the subjective probabilities). A possible example of this is the Bosnian civil war where the weakening of the Yugoslav state encouraged secession, but as a civil war ensued in Bosnia between the Muslim Bosniaks and the

Christian Serbs, outside Yugoslav forces entered the civil war on the side of the non-secessionists so deepening and probably prolonging the civil war—see Chapter 3.

5 Changes in the Subjective Rates of Discount

Mansfield and Snyder (2005) provide empirical evidence showing that immature democracies—those in the process of moving away from authoritarianism, but without a full set of democratic institutions—such as an effective opposition party, independent judiciary or a free press, are more bellicose than are well established democracies or even authoritarian countries. Their argument is that political elites in immature democracies whip up nationalist sentiment as a means of solidifying their position. In essence, this is an argument about increased expected net economic rent. However, there is a different interpretation as exemplified by a statement at the International Institute of Strategic Studies (London) by Prince zu Schwarzenberg, a Czech government representative. He stated that 'the Russians have always thought much more in long term and strategic considerations than other European states. Other European states [go] from one election to another and think more about tactics'.[4] This is an argument about the subjective rate of time preference; specifically, that mature democracies, the 'other European states', think short term relative to what the Russians do (exemplifying either dictatorship or immature democracy). Indeed, Mansfield and Snyder (2005) point out there is a marked difference between immature and mature democracies caused by the fact that governments in well-established democracies know that they will quite shortly have to face elections, while a government in an immature democracy may reason that it can postpone elections if it thinks it would lose the next one.

These arguments support the view that governments in mature democracies are more impatient for good results to place before the electorate following an act of bellicosity (an incurrence of dispute costs) than are governments of immature democracies. The latter therefore have lower rates of time preference. Thus, the 'power of discounting' over expected future economic rents is lower (higher present values) for immature democracies than it is for mature democracies.

[4] Quoted *Financial Times USA*, "Prague Warns of Kremlin Ambition", July 20, 2007, p. 4.

Mansfield and Snyder (2005) argue that: 'In democratizing states, nationalism is an ideology with tremendous appeal for elites whose privileges are threatened. It can be used to convince newly empowered constituencies that the cleavage between the privileged and the masses is unimportant compared with the cleavages that divide nations, ethnic groups or races' (p. 2). Thus, elites present arguments to the masses that increase expected non-pecuniary economic rents, backing up the argument that support for belligerence in immature democracies derives from low time preference—the expected gains from bellicosity increasing.

Another factor relating to choice of discount rate is uncertainty over post-secession quality of life. The more uncertain this is—that is, the greater is the variance of expected economic rents after secession, the higher will be the discount rate. Stein (2016) built a post-secession quality of life index composed of political rights, civil liberties, casualties of war, and economic benefits and applied it to four post-World War II secessions. These were in 1971 Bangladesh from Pakistan, in 1993 Eritrea from Ethiopia, in 2002 Timor-Leste from Indonesia, and in 2011 South Sudan from Sudan. She found no upward trends in post-secession quality of life, indicating a degree of uncertainty in expectations—which would only be true, of course, if expectations pre-secession matched this historical outcome.

6 Changes in Returns if Region B Remains in the Union

A natural resource discovery in region B will, via taxation of natural resource rents, raise the return to the Union ($y) of B remaining in the union. If the Union is cognizant of maintaining the legitimacy of the Union, it may choose to increase the return to region B (i.e., $x) through the use of subsidies. Following the beginning of North Sea oil production in Scottish waters in the 1970s, much higher per capita public spending in Scotland compared with the rest of the UK by the Union (Westminster) government is an example of a Union's attempt to increase its legitimacy in a potentially secessionist region—at the time Scotland was and remains a relatively high per capita income region in the UK.

7 More Examples of Internal Historical Sequences

As mentioned earlier, in historical time, none of the four political phases described in Figure 1 in chapter 3 need persist: tranquil unions may break apart, empires will crumble, wars of secession will come to an end, and non-resisted secessions will go through.

For an historical event to affect change, it must be numerically significant enough to change one or other of the signs of $E(NER)_B$ or $E(NER)_X$. For example, if it raises the value of $(\$rent)_t$ enough to change the sign of $E(NER)_B$ from negative to positive, region B may then pursue secession. As another example, the sign of $E(NER)_X$ may change from positive to negative as, for instance, after World War II when an exhausted UK found the *(\$persuasion cost)*$_t$ of maintaining the membership of the British Empire too great to bear, so ushering in a 'wind of change' and the dismantling of that empire.

There are twelve possible one-step events each beginning in one of the four quadrants in Fig. 1 in chapter 3 and ending in one of the other three quadrants. We will ignore the three possible sequences beginning in the southwest quadrant on the assumption that non-contested secessions go through with the effect that region B exits the Union. The remaining nine possible internal one-step histories are as follows. Possible international sequences will be discussed in the next chapter.

The nine one-step histories are as follows (in the starting point is in the lighter shaded box with the ending point in the darker shaded box, each diagram is a rendition of Fig. 1 in chapter 3.

Sequences 1–3: Beginning with* Tranquility *the movement can be to:

Internal (or societal) warfare as in Fig. 1 is the largest single category of warfare since the end of World War II as is identified by Pettersson et al. (2019) and earlier by Marshall and Gurr (2005). The other two are

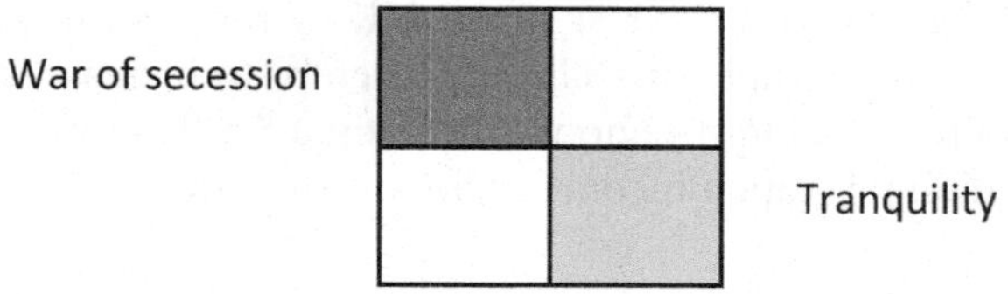

Fig. 1 War of secession (SE to NW) (*Source* Author's creation)

'interstate including colonial' and 'interstate'. Not all societal warfare is for secession, but in many instances it is—the other type being for control of a state's political machinery. Colonial warfare corresponds exactly with our modeling of 'secession from empire'.

Gurr (2000) notes a trend in the 1990s for Unions to prevent wars of secession by anticipating the demands of ethnic minorities for greater access to state power, ethnic recognition, or autonomy. This may be interpreted as 'human rights' being given greater recognition to head off conflict. Kissinger (1994) argues that adherence to Basket III, recognition of human rights, by signatories of the Helsinki Accords (1975) played a significant role in the breakup of the Soviet Empire less than two decades later. Greater autonomy leaves region B with more economic rent—$E(NEB)_B$ increases. The Union X is trading off lower persuasion cost for lower economic rent for itself. As a result, $E(NEB)_X$ may rise or fall. As discussed in Chapter 3, there are many recent and ongoing examples of wars of secession.

There are examples of non-resisted secession; Norway from Sweden in 1905 is a case in point as is Montenegro from Yugoslavia in 2006, see Fig. 2 below. There are also 'partial secessions'—a move to become internally self-governing—by 14 British Overseas Territories in 2002—as pointed out in chapter 3 (Fig. 2).

A tranquil relationship may exist between region B and the Union of which it is part see Fig. 3 below. Perhaps B had sought X's protection by joining it. But once B became a member of the Union, the Union may begin to exploit B and be prepared to use force to prevent B seceding. Thus, B becomes a part of an empire. Kryzanek (2000, p. 30) reflects the well-known argument that through the Monroe Doctrine (1823), the USA set itself up as the protector of South America from European

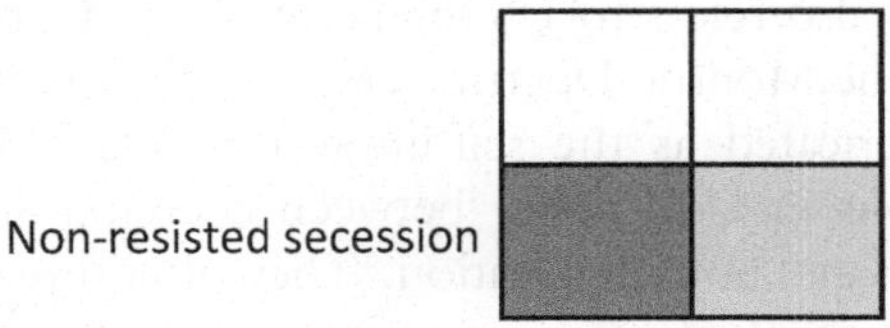

Fig. 2 Non-resisted secession (SE to SW) (*Source* Author's creation)

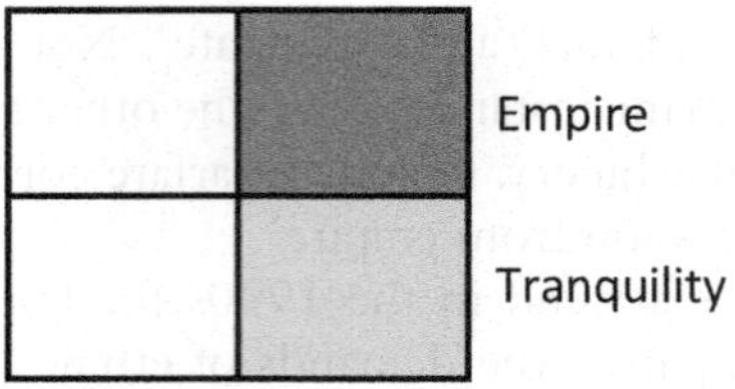

Fig. 3 Empire (SE to NE) (*Source* Author's creation)

incursions; and the USA was among the first country to recognize the independence of the newly proclaimed South American Republics. If it was that the USA had no designs on South American countries yet had them in its sphere of influence, the main aim being to keep the Europeans out, it could be said that a condition of ***tranquility*** existed between them. Smith (1995) sees the application of the Monroe Doctrine in South America as largely benign but only until such time as the USA started to intervene there in its own interests. Similarly, Knight (2005) argues that 'for decades the Monroe Doctrine was a mere rhetorical document'. The case of Chile rather bears out the argument that the Monroe Doctrine has been used as a cover for the pursued of US national interests. In 1973, after free elections in Chile, the USA inserted a US-leaning dictator when it appeared possible that Chile would leave its sphere of influence. This latter sequence can be characterized as Chile moving from tranquility to a subordinate position in an empire. Gilderhus (2006) makes similar arguments. He describes how the US 'good neighbor' policy toward South America changed with the rise of communism in the post-World War II period. In Guatemala in 1954, the USA sponsored a clandestine invasion against a new government that it saw as being against US interests. That government was overthrown, and the ensuing 40-year civil war cost 100,000 lives. He too also refers to US interventions in Cuba and Chile and concludes that: 'The Monroe Doctrine consistently served what U.S. leaders defined or fabricated as the self-interest of the USA and also reflected the oscillations in U.S. policy between coercion and cooperation and intervention and nonintervention. They also revealed a sense of ignorance and built-in condescension toward Latin Americans, often regarded as inferiors on racial grounds. No wonder that so many Latin American radicals and nationalists historically have looked upon the USA as their natural enemy' (p. 16).

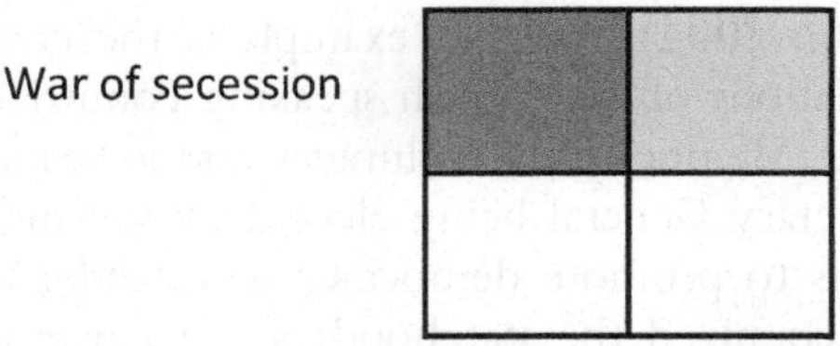

Fig. 4 War of secession (NE to NW) (*Source* Author's creation)

Sequences 4–6: Beginning with* Empire *the movement can be to:
For example, in Fig. 4 Chechens fought a war of secession with Russia as well as several examples are shown in Fig. 2 in chapter 3.

There are several examples of non-resisted secession as shown in Fig. 5 drawn from the British Empire once it was recognized in the 1950s that there was a 'wind of change'. For example, neither Ghana or Nigeria had to fight a war of secession to gain independence.

A case in Fig. 6 is exemplified by the granting of greater governmental autonomy to the British colonies in Canada to manage their own affairs—a system of colonial governance that originated in the 1838 Durham Report and in the same century spread to Australia and New Zealand

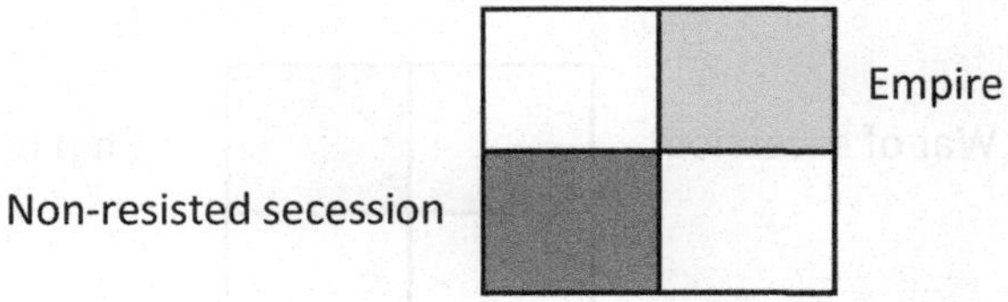

Fig. 5 Non-resisted secession (NE to SW) (*Source* Author's creation)

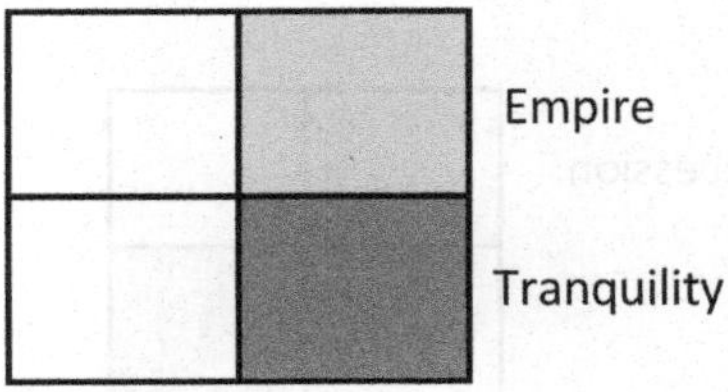

Fig. 6 Tranquility (NE to SE) (*Source* Author's creation)

(Lucas 1912; Ferguson 2004). Another example is the creation of the Commonwealth of Nations of 54 English speaking countries out of the former British Empire. Membership is voluntary and is headquartered in London with its Secretary General being elected by the member countries. The main aim is to promote democracy worldwide; for example, in 1972 it quickly recognized the statehood of the newly independent Bangladesh. It amounts to what is a loose grouping of countries.

Sequences 7–9: Beginning with* War of Secession *Movement Can Be to:

Chechens in losing their war of secession had to accept remaining as a sub-nation in an empire—Russia's (Fig. 7). All secessionist wars that do not lead to independence and do not satisfy sub-nation demands end this way. Chechnya in the space of about a dozen years therefore passed through the sequence of colony of USSR, war of secession, defeat, and then colony of Russia.

According to Gurr (2000), 'In recent wars of self-determination fighting usually began with demands for complete independence and ended with negotiated or de facto autonomy within the state' (p. 57, see Fig. 8). Examples include Northern Ireland's 1998 Good Friday Agreement between the UK and Republic of Ireland governments; the agreement between Macedonian Albanians—who had been supporting the

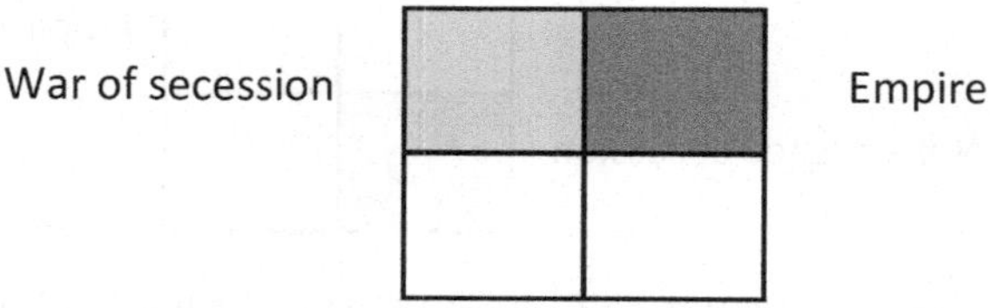

Fig. 7 Empire (NW to NE) (*Source* Author's creation)

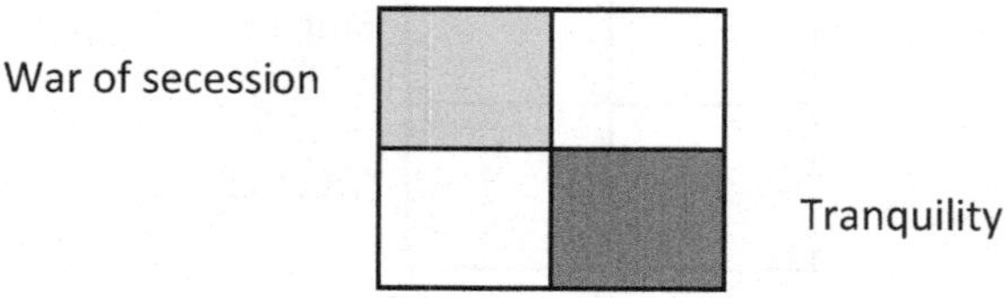

Fig. 8 Tranquility (NW to SE) (*Source* Author's creation)

Macedonian Liberation Army and the Macedonian government in 2001; and the Mizoram Peace Accord of 1986 between the Mizo National Front and the government of India. In 1966, the Mizoram National Front, with the support of East Pakistan (which became Bangladesh), began an armed insurgency to secede from India and to create the sovereign state of Greater Mizoram. According to Sharma (2016), the desire for secession stemmed from the Mizoram people's alienation from the people of the Indian state of Assam. The dispute was settled in 1986 with the granting of separate statehood to Mizoram, but continuing as part of India.

Harris (2010) also discusses a case where a secessionist dispute was settled when both sides compromised on their war objectives. The case in question is that of the Aceh, a province of Indonesia, where the secessionist GAM had been fighting against forces deployed by the government of Indonesia that aimed to prevent secession. After the humanitarian crisis caused by the Aceh tsunami of 2004, Harris argues that neither side wanted to prolong that humanitarian crisis by engaging in further hostilities. The GAM agreed to regional autonomy, or, devolution of internal government to Aceh that was offered by the government of Indonesia. Both sides therefore got a portion of what they had been fighting for, a degree of independence for the people of Aceh and retention of Aceh within the state of Indonesia (Fig. 9).

This is a successful war of secession but followed by a peace treaty in which the Union recognizes B's independence in international law. An example of this is the American War of Independence which was effectively over in early-1781 followed by the Treaty of Paris that became effective in 1784.

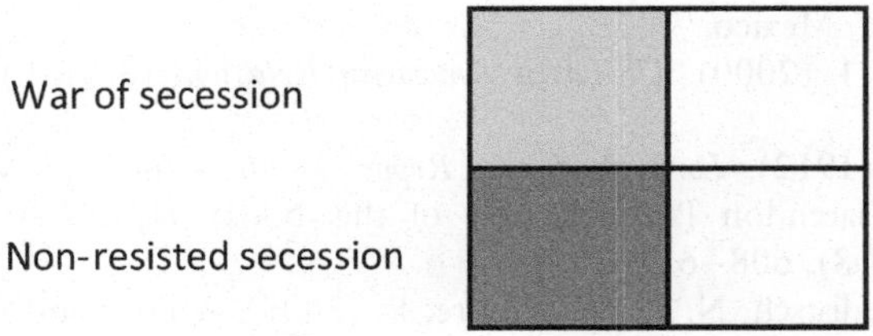

Fig. 9 Secession (NW to SW) (*Source* Author's creation)

8 Conclusions

This chapter has discussed the drivers of historical sequences as set out in Table 1. All four of the possible starting points assumed that B is a region in the Union X. The nine possible one-step historical sequences describe B's progress in either exiting a Union or remaining as a region in it. Examples of each of the nine possible movements are given, but the author welcomes other interpretations.

The next chapter shows how our fundamental economic model can be used to highlight interstate (between state) rivalries.

References

Blattman, C., & Annan, J. (2010). The Consequences of Child Soldiering. *The Review of Economics and Statistics, 92*(4), 882–898.

Collier, P., & Hoeffler, A. (2000). *Greed and Grievance in Civil War*, Policy Research Working Paper 2355, World Bank.

Ferguson, N. (2004). *Empire: How Britain Made the Modern World*. Harmondsworth: Penguin Books.

Gilderhus, M. T. (2006). The Monroe Doctrine: Meanings and Implications. *Presidential Studies Quarterly, 36*(1), 5–16.

Gurr, T. R. (2000, May/June). Ethnic Warfare on the Wane. *Foreign Affairs, 79*(3), 52–64.

Harris, A. (2010). Separatist Insurgency, Objective Referents and Autonomy. *Cooperation and Conflict, 45*(4), 387–405.

Kissinger, H. (1994). *Diplomacy*. New York: Simon and Schuster.

Knight, A. (2005). US Imperialism/Hegemony and Latin American Resistance, Workshop on *Empire and Dissent: US Hegemony in Latin America*, Program on Global Security and Cooperation at the Social Science Research Council, Cuernavaca, Mexico.

Kryzanek, M. J. (2000). *US-Latin American Relations* (3rd ed.). New Haven: Praeger.

Lucas, C. P. (1912). *Lord Durham's Report on the Affairs of North America*. Oxford: Clarendon Press. Review of this book: *The American Historical Review, 18*(3), 608–611.

Lujala, P., Gledistsch, N. P., & Gilmore, E. (2005). A Diamond Curse? *Journal of Conflict Resolution, 49*(4), 538–562.

Mansfield, E. D., & Snyder, J. (2005). *Why Emerging Democracies Go to War*. Cambridge: MIT Press.

Marshall, M. G., & Gurr, T. R. (2005). *Peace and Conflict*, Chapter 2, The Peace and Conflict Ledger: Country Ratings of Peace-Building Capacity in 2005.

Center for International Development and Conflict Management, University of Maryland. http://members.aol.com/cspmgm/PC2005.pdf.

Pettersson, T., Hogbladh, S., & Oberg, M. (2019). Organized Violence 1989–2018 and Peace Agreements. *Journal of Peace Research, 56*(4), 589–603.

Riall, L. (1994). *The Italian Risorgimento: State, Society, and National Unification*. London: Routledge.

Sen, A. (2006). *Identity and Violence: The Illusion of Destiny*. New York: Norton.

Sharma S. K. (2016, June). *Lessons from Mizoram Insurgency and Peace Accord 1986*, Vivekananda International Foundation, Occasional Paper.

Smith, G. (1995). *The Last Years of the Monroe Doctrine*. New York: Hill and Wang.

Stein, C. (2016). *Successful Secessionist Movements and the Uncertainty of Post-Secession Quality of Life*. https://ir.library.oregonstate.edu/concern/honors_college_theses/c247dv15r.

CHAPTER 5

International Sequencing with Historical Examples

Abstract The basic economic model developed in Chapters 2 and 3 is now applied to interstate sequencing. The benefit-cost analysis again shows that there are two stable equilibria and two transitional dis-equilibria. Three interstate historical sequences are identified and examples of each are discussed.

Keywords Clash of civilizations · End of history · Harmony · Independence · War

1 Introduction

Historical events in *international sequencing* can also be described using the economic model laid out in Chapters 2 and 3. In this chapter, it is assumed that B is an *independent country* (as defined in international law under the Montevideo Convention on the Rights and Duties of States, 1933) separate from another country, country X.[1] These historical sequences are described in Fig. 1 where the combinations of the signs of $E(NER)_B$ and $E(NER)_X$ in the respective quadrants are the same as Fig. 1

[1] This chapter recognizes that the concept of independence can have 'shades of grey'—for example, if in an ongoing secessionist war, one or just a few outside powers recognized the independence of the secessionists as having their own independent state.

P. Hallwood, *Interpreting Historical Sequences Using Economic Models*,
https://doi.org/10.1007/978-3-030-53854-5_5

COUNTRY X	COUNTRY B: Independence preferred	COUNTRY B: Incorporation into X accepted
X threatens B's independence	$E(NER)_B > 0$ **War:** X attempts to takeover B $E(NER)_X > 0$	$E(NER)_B < 0$ **X takes over B with little resistance** $E(NER)_X > 0$
X does not threaten B's independence	$E(NER)_B > 0$ **B as an independent country** $E(NER)_X < 0$	$E(NER)_B < 0$ **Harmony:** B may approach X to join its Union $E(NER)_X < 0$

Fig. 1 Will B remain independent? (*Source* Author's creation)

in chapter 3. The questions now are: 'is country B better off remaining independent of country X?' And 'will country X be better off or not if it "absorbs" country B?'. It is understood that country B will remain as an independent country as long as $E(NER)_B > 0$ and $E(NER)_X < 0$—this is in the southwest box of Fig. 1. Country B wishes to remain independent and it would resist incorporation into country X and, at the same time, country X has no designs on B to incorporate it into its own Union.

A word about B 'remaining an independent country' is in order. Losing independence can mean the incorporation of B into the Union X. For example, the re-incorporation of Catalonia into Spain at the end of the Spanish War of Succession in 1714. Or, incorporation of B into the Union X also applies to colonialism where the colony does not become part of the 'mother country' X.

The southwest box in Fig. 1 is the natural starting point as all three historical sequences leading away from it are common in recorded history.

All the historical movements again begin in the lighter shaded box and move to the darker shaded box.

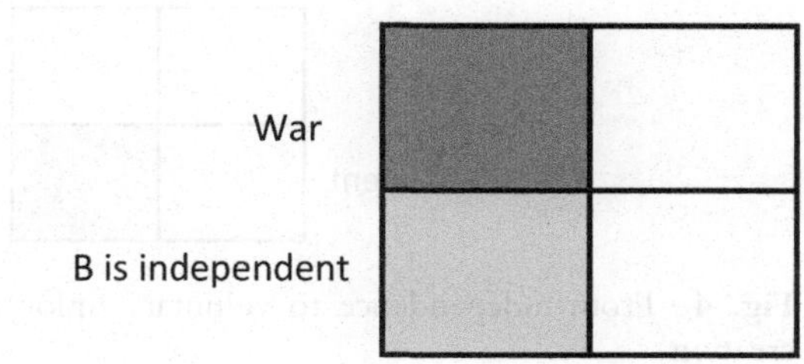

Fig. 2 Warring nations (SW to NW) (*Source* Author's creation)

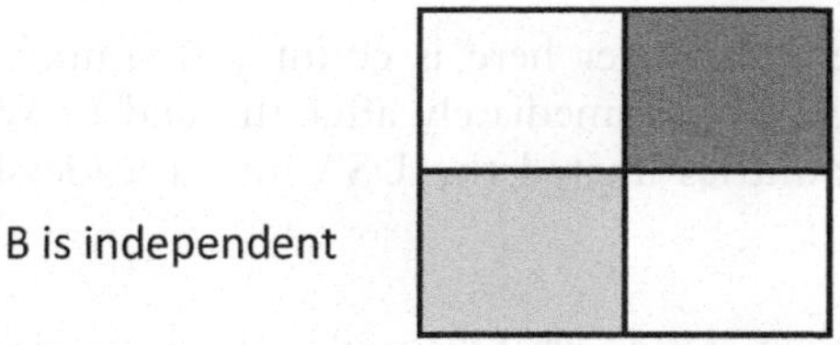

Fig. 3 Empire (SW to NE) (*Source* Author's creation)

2 Three Main Sequences

If $E(NER)_X$ turns from negative to positive, the historical sequence is to the northwest box. Country X wishes to incorporate country B, but country B wishes to remain independent. Thus, see Fig. 2.

This is the case of ***international war*** over control of territory such as Germany's invasions of Czechoslovakia and Poland in 1939. There are many such other examples in European history.

Secondly, see Fig. 3.

This is incorporation of formerly independent country B into country X's wider Union with little or no resistance by B, the sign of $E(NER)_B$ being negative. There are many historical examples of this sequence, southwest to northeast as it includes the rise European colonial Empires of Spain, Portugal, the UK, France, and the Netherlands.[2] To the extent that there was some resistance by B, the move from B's independence in the southwest box of Fig. 1 is via a brief visit to the northwest box.

Thirdly, see Fig. 4.

An independent country B voluntarily joins country X, or else a Union led by country X, while country X has no desire to involve itself militarily

[2] On the Inca's ready submission to Spain in the sixteenth century, see Madariaga (1948).

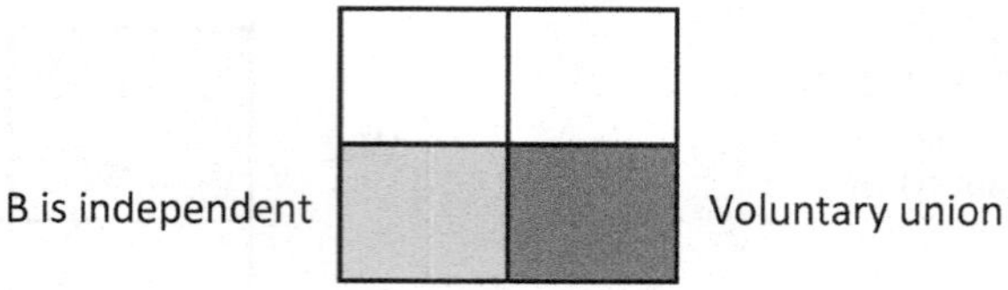

Fig. 4 From independence to voluntary union (SW to SE) (*Source* Author's creation)

with country B. The first mover here is country B. Lundestad (1986) argues that in the five years immediately after the end of World War II Western European countries invited the USA into a leadership position and he concludes that:

> this American expansion created what we could call an American empire, this was to a large extent an empire by invitation.

This is 'harmony'. The most obvious current example of this historical sequence is the continuing enlargement of the European Union as the still recently liberated countries of Eastern Europe hastened to join it. Scotland's incorporation into the UK also falls into this category when in 1707 it willingly joined that Union of countries.

Rising powers and war. Another case that fits into Fig. 1 is when country B is the instigator of war. This can happen when country B attacks country X because the latter is seen to be acting to suppress country B's economic and regional hegemonic development. Monteiro and Debs (2019) illustrate this case with Japan's attack on the USA in 1941, pointing out that a relatively weak country may choose to start a war with a strong country. They argue that Japan was trying to develop a 'sphere of influence' in Asia through which to source raw materials and into which to sell its products, thereby strengthening its economic and potential military power, but that US foreign policy opposed this, an opposition that would have held back Japan's economic and regional hegemonic development.

The novelty of this argument is that war can happen when an existing hegemon, country X—the USA, acts, or, is expected to act, to hold country B, Japan, back from access to the raw materials and foreign markets it needs for its economic development. It is country B's weakness rather than its strength that is the cause of war because greater access to raw materials and foreign markets translates into an expected large increase in country B's net economic rents, i.e., $E(NER)_B$ is large; if country B already had such access the increase in its expected economic rents would not be so large. This argument though supposes that country B's dispute costs will not be too great, which in the Japan-US case was a serious miscalculation by Japan.

Monteiro and Debs (2019) also argue that even if a hegemon did not want to constrain the rise of a competitor nation it has a 'commitment problem'. That is, even if a hegemon says it will not interfere with the economic and, therefore, potential military rise of country B it cannot believably commit *not* one day to interfere. In turn, country B fears 'hold up' such that the hegemon may indeed act to prevent it getting a fair economic return on the sunk costs it has incurred in investing in infrastructure to source raw materials from third countries.

It follows from this that war is less prevalent in an open world economy—one promoted by international institutions such as the UN, WTO, IMF, World Bank, because rising powers are not prevented from accessing the imported resources and markets they need to increase their rates of economic growth (see Crescenzi 2003; McDonald 2009; Powell 2006). An open world economy therefore acts as a commitment device because leading powers will not want to upset the international system of which they are a major part.

3 Comparison with Other Models

The model set out in Fig. 1 incorporates three recently developed historical models—the optimal country size model of Alesina and Spolaore (2003), the 'end of history' arguments of Fukuyama (1992), and the 'clash of civilizations' reasoning of Huntington (1993).

The main thrust of the discussion of Alesina and Spolaore (2003) work in Chapter 4 is that they correctly identify several exogenous events that can lead to secession but that the 'real world' is not quite as simple as they suppose because secessionists may have to get over the hump of resistance to secession by the Union of which they are a part. It is the case therefore that the strength of historical drivers has to be large enough to get over these resistances—as thresholds have to be crossed secessions may be delayed, possibly for a long time.

A factor that can work in the opposite direction raising, or, at least, maintaining the optimal size of countries, is the introduction of a workable governmental system of federalism. Such a system reduces $E(NER)_B$—deriving from an increase in $\$x_t$ (as regions have greater scope to create and retain economic rents within their locality). Scotland in the UK effectively retaining the tax revenues derived from North Sea offshore oil production beginning the 1970s is a case in point—see Chapter 8. And on a more challenging level are the ongoing attempts to design an acceptable system of fiscal federalism in the European Union so as to encourage 'ever closer union'.

3.1 *The End of History?*

It can also be claimed that our model considers more fundamental details than does the 'end of history' reasoning of Fukuyama (1992). He asserts that once liberal democracy is widely practiced around the globe historical sequences will come to an end because democracies do not fight democracies. He points to general agreement on the validity of liberal democracy as a form of government because the philosophy of liberal democracy does not have internal contradictions, making it the end point of ideological progression. The 'victory' of liberal democracy will therefore establish internal tranquility in the southeast boxes of Fig. 1 in chapter 3 and international harmony as in Fig. 1.

He explains the ending of historical sequences based on the philosophical proposition that the same values as expressed in systems of liberal democracy are generally accepted around the world, while competing political philosophies such as of communism, fascism, or monarchial governance they are not. Most importantly, liberal democracies supply mutual recognition of human values and this he argues is sufficient for peace to hold overtime—mutual recognition of each other's worth happens because of shared values.

In the framework of this book, 'mutual recognition of worth' within a state means that the people of a perhaps once disadvantaged region B do not wish to either secede to set up their own state, one where they are not looked down upon; or, to revolt with the aim of gaining greater political representation in the state of which they are apart.

The form of recognition that Fukuyama has in mind does not exist in societies that have a master and a 'slave' class—a class of people whose worth is not recognized as being 'equal' by the ruling class. The problem with dictatorships that has led to their frequent downfall is that so often large parts of their populations are not recognized for their equal worth as contributors to society; there is no mutual recognition of worth in a philosophical sense rather than in their marginal products of labor being equal. Given this, Fukuyama argues that the ruled-over eventually come to press for the creation of new political systems in which they are recognized as equal citizens. As it is only liberal democracies that can supply this mutual recognition, once liberal democracies have taken over the world there will be an end of history.

There is a good deal to like about Fukuyama's philosophy-based analysis of the 'end of history' because his arguments align with the notion that economic rents, especially a component calculated as willingness to pay for 'recognition', are similar with or without secession. But to talk about an end of history, even on his terms, is premature. As Hobson (2015) argues 'the rise of China, combined with Russia's bullish behavior and the problems of established democracies following the 2008 financial crisis, all point towards the weakening of the West's … hegemony' (p. 204). Most obviously the world is not made up of liberal democracies 'high' on mutual recognition; there are still many despotic countries including China and Russia, and many in Africa and the Middle East. And while it is true that international wars are relatively infrequent, civil wars, especially in Africa, are an ongoing occurrence.

It can also be argued that even if liberal democracies 'took over the world' history would still not end. The work of Alesina and Spolaore (2003) gives some reasons as to why this might not be the case. In a world free of international war, our catch all 'region B' might want to seceded from the Union of which it is a part—with world peace breaking out the security benefits of being part of a larger Union become smaller and secession can become a desired choice, Scotland from the UK is a possible example. Similarly, the spread of free trade across the globe can encourage secessionist desires because access to large domestic markets becomes less essential for regional prosperity.

In the other direction, there is the possible recombination of independent countries into a single federalist system, which is an aim in some political quarters for the members of the European Union. This could happen with the development and general acceptance of a workable architecture of federal governance, an architecture that at minimum must include an acceptable system of regional representation, and the sharing of the financial burdens of government. Put differently, in Fig. 1, the 'end of history' could happen with harmony between separate nations, in the southeast box, but this is not to conclude that even tranquil nations will not want to recombine into some other form of governmental arrangements.

3.2 *Clash of Civilizations*

The main similarity between Fukuyama's 'end of history' and Huntington's (1993) 'clash of civilizations' is that the significant variable in both models is economic rent as measured by willingness to pay for some cultural or political values. But, it might be noted, in neither approach are other significant variables relevant to historical sequences included—specifically dispute and persuasion costs, time preferences and how many years forward looking are the potential combatants.

The main difference between these two models is that in the 'end of history' view countries around the world come to value the same thing—the mutual regard promoted by liberal democracy; while in the 'clash of civilizations' cultural differences persist and these might prevent the spread of liberal democracy around the globe. According to Huntington (1993), 'a civilization is the highest cultural grouping of people and the broadest level of cultural identity' (p. 24). He identified nine main civilizations that span the globe—Western, Orthodox Christian, Islamic, Buddhist, Hindu, African, Latin American, Sinic, and Japanese. It is these cultural differences that were seen by Huntington as promoting international rivalries.

Take the case of Chinese hegemony in East Asia which Huntington foresaw in the early-1990s as a likely historical development: countries such as South Korea and Japan would come to accept this so giving up their support for US leadership in the region. In terms of Fig. 1 assume that China is country X and South Korea is country B. As of 2020 they reside in the southwest box of Fig. 1 with X not threatening B's independence while B (South Korea) wishes to remain independent of X. However, with the rise of China's political, economic and military powers, X (China) comes to want to incorporate B (South Korea) into its sphere of influence (the sign of $E(NER)_X$ turning from negative to positive), and B, seeing the rise of X comes to choose not to resist incorporation into X's sphere of influence. The latter would be especially so if the USA gave up its already weakening hegemony in East Asia. Thus, for country B, $E(NER)_B$ turns from positive to negative implying that it will not resist

X's hegemony and the system in East Asia moves from the southwest to the northeast box.

Huntington (1993) also identified 'cleft' countries that were and are home for peoples of different cultures. Many of these are found in sub-Saharan Africa that combine Islamic and non-Islamic cultures. It is, of course, in countries such as these where civil war can and does breakout between the peoples of the different cultures, an analysis of which was offered in Chapter 3.

4 Conclusions

This chapter has applied the basic economic model developed in Chapters 2 and 3 to the international sphere and it has emphasized three major international historical situations: warring nations, empire and joining together in a voluntary union. It has also been shown that the 'end of history' and 'clash of civilizations' arguments on international sequencing are special cases that are easily fitted into the more general model developed in this book.

References

Alesina and Spolaore. (2003). *The Size of Nations*. Cambridge: MIT Press.

Crescenzi, M. J. C. (2003). Economic Exit, Interdependence, and Conflict. *Journal of Politics, 65*(3), 809–832.

de Madariaga, S. (1948). *The Fall of the Spanish American Empire*. NewYork: MacMillan Company.

Fukuyama, F. (1992). *The End of History and the Last Man*. New York: Free Press.

Hobson, C. (2015). *The Rise of Democracy: Revolution, War and Transformations in International Politics since 1776*. Edinburgh: Edinburgh University Press.

Huntington, S. (1993). The Clash of Civilizations? *Foreign Affairs, 72*(3), 22–50.

Lundestad, G. (1986). Empire by Invitation? The United States and Western Europe, 1945–1952. *Journal of Peace Research, 23*(3), 263–277.

McDonald, P. J. (2009). *The Invisible Hand of Peace: Capitalism, the War Machine, and International Relations Theory*. Ithaca: Cornell University Press.

Monteiro, N. P., & Debs, A. (2019). An Economic Theory of War. *The Journal of Political Science, 82*(1), 255–268.

Powell, R. (2006). War as a Commitment Problem. *International Organization, 60*(1), 169–203.

CHAPTER 6

Peacekeeping and Sequencing

Abstract Successful peacekeeping missions led by the UN, the Africa Union, NATO, and other organizations are framed as speeding up historical sequences that might otherwise flag for lack of trust between the opposing parties. It is explained that while UN Security Council sanctioned peacekeeping minimizes free-riding, there are political constraints on both how much money is available and which missions the Council will approve. With other peacekeeping organizations free riding is an empirically acknowledged problem; the characteristics required for peacekeeping arrangements to be 'self-enforcing' are discussed.

Keywords African union · Free riding · NATO · Peacekeeping · Peacemaking · UN

1 Introduction

The focus in this chapter is on how peacekeeping can help to end hostilities by either promoting secession of a sub-nation group from an existing state, or, by bringing the different sides to live peacefully together in a reformed state. The 'how' in this chapter is discussed in terms of the fundamental sequencing model introduced in Chapter 3.

Peacekeeping is aimed at bringing tranquility to a nation that has been at war with itself or else it enables secession of a sub-nation group from it.

P. Hallwood, *Interpreting Historical Sequences Using Economic Models*,
https://doi.org/10.1007/978-3-030-53854-5_6

It is also used to dampen interstate conflicts. Peacekeeping is a process put in place once hostilities have diminished but could quite easily reignite. The main peacekeeping organizations are the UN, NATO, the African Union, and other self-selecting groups of countries. While peacekeeping missions always list several objectives, the principal aim, implicitly at least, is to reduce the probability of reversion to war. Peacemaking is related to peacekeeping but is used when a war is still going on at a more intense level than is the case with peacekeeping. It can be said that the aim of peacemaking is to move the combatants to a stage where peacekeepers can move in. Unfortunately, there are constraints on the effectiveness of peacekeeping missions that can stem from organizational or financial limitations.

This chapter proceeds in Sect. 2 with description of the extent of peacekeeping around the world. Section 3 offers a discussion of peacekeeping in the sequential framework of multi-nation development introduced in Chapter 3. Section 4 discusses what peacekeepers need to target to be effective. Section 5 discusses UN peacekeeping and the various constraints that limit its effectiveness. In Sect. 6, it is recognized that peacekeeping missions are expensive 'businesses' that supply public goods—'peace' and humanitarian aid among them. The financing of UN missions is not seriously reduced by free riding because of the way the UN is financed, but other types financing problems do exist. NATO and other non-UN missions are subject to free riding and a discussion of free riding is offered. Section 7 discusses what factors can help to limit free riding. Section 8 draws conclusions.

2 Peacekeeping Around the World

About 1.5 billion people live in conflict zones (Autesserre 2019). The UN was operating 15 multilateral peacekeeping and special political operations in 2020 deploying over 98,000 personnel drawn from 120 countries. UN peacekeeping missions account for two-thirds of all peacekeeping personnel with almost three-quarters of all personnel (including non-UN personnel) working in Africa. UN peacekeeping costs were \$6.8 billion in 2019. From its first mission in 1948 to 2019 the UN has operated 70 missions. There have been 39 non-UN peacekeeping missions. Ongoing UN peacekeeping operations are in Cyprus, Kosovo, Afghanistan, Kashmir, the Golan Heights, Iraq, Lebanon, the Democratic Republic of Congo, Darfur, Mali, Western Sahara, Abyei, Central

African Republic, and South Sudan. The African Union has peacekeeping missions in Somalia—the largest single multinational peacekeeping action, and in the Central African Republic. Africa 'hosted' eight of the ten largest peacekeeping missions, accounting for most of global peacekeeping personnel.[1] NATO has ongoing peacekeeping missions in Kosovo and Afghanistan, and it operated one in Bosnia 1992–2004. Some other peacekeeping forces that have ceased operation include India's forces in Sri Lanka (1987–1990), an international force led by Australia in East Timor, 1999–2000, and Economic Community of West African States Monitoring Group that operated in Liberia 1990–1995 and again in 2003, in the Sierra Leone civil war of 1997–2000, in Guinea-Bissau in 1999 and on the Guinea-Liberia border in 2001.

Other categories of peacekeeping missions include coalitions of like-minded countries combining to achieve a common objective—such as Kosovo's secession from Serbia where a UN civilian administration worked with NATO peacekeeping forces (see Visoka et al. 2020). Hybrid peacekeeping missions include the joint of operations of NATO and the Organization for Security and Cooperation in Europe (O.S.C.E.) in Bosnia and Herzegovina beginning in 1996, and the NATO-African Union Mission in Somalia where NATO provides strategic air and planning support.[2] There are also UN Trust Fund missions providing, e.g., humanitarian assistance in Somalia in support of the African Union Mission in Somalia (A.M.I.S.O.N.)—see UN Support Office, that are not covered by UN general assessments, rather they are financed by voluntary contributions for specific peacekeeping purposes.[3]

Most of these peacekeeping missions were and are aimed at ending intrastate violence—in the terminology of this book, to bring 'tranquility'. However, several peacekeeping missions have promoted secession of a sub-nation group from a larger multi-nation unit. Examples are NATO's

[1] Stockholm International Peace Institute, *Global and regional trends in multilateral peace operations*, 2008–2017, https://www.sipri.org/commentary/topical-backgrounder/2018/global-and-regional-trends-multilateral-peace-operations-2008–2017.

[2] See http://amisom-au.org/wp-content/uploads/2008/09/AMISOM-Mandate-extended-to-Oct.-2012.pdf and http://www.cfr.org/africa/african-peacekeeping-operations/p9333#p6.

[3] This listing of peacekeepers and peacekeeping locations is not meant to be comprehensive, rather just to give an indication of the global extent of peacekeeping and what are the peacekeeping organizations.

involvement in the secession of Kosovo from Serbia in 2008; South Sudan from Sudan in 2011; and Eritrea's internationally monitored vote on independence leading to its separation from Ethiopia in 1993. Two disputes that had elements of secession in them but were overtaken by other events are Abyei's UN monitored vote on choosing whether to remain part of Sudan or to join South Sudan, and the Movement for the Liberation of Azawad calling for the secession of northern Mali from Mali in 2012. Also, UN peacekeeping in 1962 had led to the suppression of Katanga's secession from Congo.

3 Understanding the Objectives of Peacekeeping

To analyze the sequential dynamics of peacekeeping, Fig. 1 from chapter 3 is reproduced here as Fig. 1 with two modifications relevant to peacekeeping operations. These modifications are necessary because peacekeeping happens before historical sequences have worked themselves through. It will be recalled from Chapter 3 that a 'Union' is a state with three subsidiary regions, A, B, and C (it could be more). For whatever reason, region B is motivated to secede from the Union. The first modification is that it is also possible that region B fights not to secede but

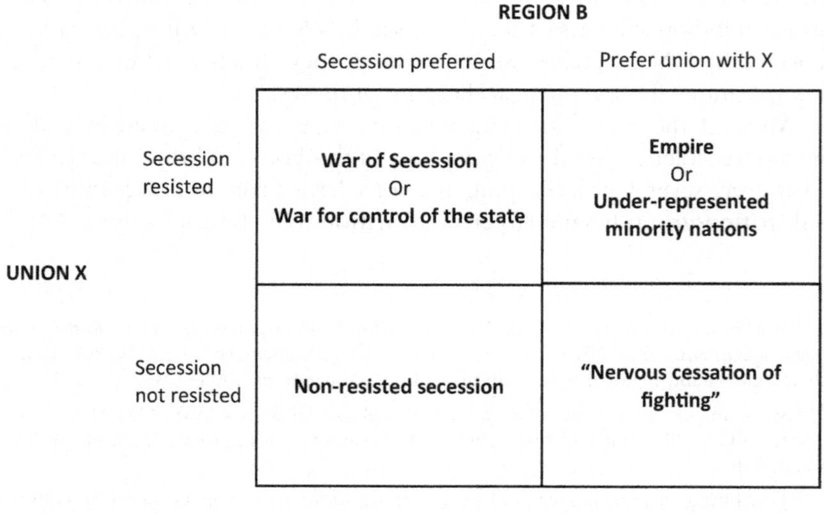

Fig. 1 Sequences in the presence of peacekeeping (*Source* Author's creation)

to gain control of the Union (as is the case, for example with Islamists in both Mali and Somalia), or, at least, to increase representation in national-level politics. In the latter case, region B fights to rid itself from the shackles of 'Empire'. Peacekeeping is meant to hurry along historical sequences to just conclusions that may otherwise be frustrated by a lack of trust between the opposing sides.

The second modification recognizes that peacekeeping begins after fighting has diminished. 'Tranquility' though is an over-statement because if peacekeepers are needed, the situation is better described as a 'nervous cessation of fighting'. Even so, outright war has stopped for an interval of time and the aim of the peacekeepers is to increase the length of this and, ultimately, to discourage reversion to war.

If secession does eventually occur the progression will have passed through the stages of war of secession to nervous cessation of fighting and on to non-resisted secession. The case of South Sudan from Sudan is a case in point. A UN mission in the Sudan began in 2005 with the *Comprehensive Peace Agreement* (CPA) aimed at maintaining a ceasefire, disarmament, and provision of humanitarian aid. It was signed by the Sudanese government and the rebel Sudan People's Liberation Movement. The two sides had for decades fought over natural resources, political power, the role of religion in the state, and self-determination for national minorities. The UN mission led to the referendum in 2011 and the secession of South Sudan.

By contrast, the UN's Interim Security Force for Abyei, set up in June 2011 and running at least to 2020, has not lead to the secession of Abyei from Sudan to South Sudan or even to a vote by the inhabitants on whether to remain as part of Sudan or to secede to South Sudan. The conflict there is between the government of Sudan and Abyei's Sudan People's Liberation Movement-North. With the split of South Sudan from Sudan in 2011, the people of Abyei had been given hope of a referendum in which they would decide the region's future. However, the Sudanese government has prevented a referendum taking place.

4 Peacekeeping: Fundamentals of Effectiveness

Four mechanisms through which peacekeeping works are identified by Fortna (2008). These are: by changing the combatants' ***incentives*** away from war and toward peace; by reducing their ***uncertainty*** about each other's intensions, that is improving ***trust***; by preventing ***accidents*** that could restart war; and by preventing *exclusion* of interested parties from the peacemaking process. Howard (2008) also argues that peacekeepers aim to directly influence the preferences of political leaders—what Fortna categorized as 'incentives'.

These mechanisms clearly relate to the analytical framework laid out in Chapters 2, 3, and 4.[4] With the variables set out in Table 1 in chapter 4 in mind the following arguments can be made about how successful peacekeeping missions come about.

First, there is the very broad category of 'changing the combatants' *incentives* away from war and towards peace'. A successful outcome here can involve moving any combinations of the 6 variables that affect region B's incentives for prolonging war with the Union of which it is a part; similarly, with the six variables that influence a Union's incentives to prolong war. To be more specific:

1. With peacekeeping troops on the ground, peacekeeping is likely aimed at raising both region B's dispute costs and the Union's persuasion costs (This corresponds to line 1 in Table 1 in chapter 4). These costs of war are raised if, with the peacekeepers standing between the two sides, reversion to war could well be met by military resistance by the peacekeepers (as well as the other side of the initial civil war). This point suggests that well-armed peacekeepers can be a vital input to achieving peace. The costs of war for both sides can also be raised if foreign aid is withdrawn if there was a reversion to fighting.
2. In the case of a possible secession, say, Kosovo from Serbia, peacekeepers should try to maintain in the minds of the leaders of the Union that region B will secede. That is, Pr_t, the Union's subjective probability of region B seceding, is high (see Table 1 in chapter 4, line 3). If this probability fell enough, perhaps because of adverse events in region B (e.g., its respected leader died, its supply of arms dried up, or, the peacekeepers were seen as being ineffective),

[4]In Chapter 2, see Eqs. 1 to 4 that lay out a secessionist groups net gains from secession, or, in the context of this chapter, the net gains of an 'out' sub-nation group from gaining better political representation at the national level. Similarly, in Chapter 2 see Eqs. 5 to 7 that define a Union's net gains from preventing secession of a sub-nation group, or, if the fight is over control of the state, preventing the sub-national group obtaining a greater political voice at the national level.

the Union's net expected benefit from renewing war could increase enough to move it all the way back to war with the aim of 'Empire' (a counter historical example would be Kosovo's reabsorption into Serbia).

3. Peacekeepers may act to lower a Union's rate of return (its economic rents) if region B remained 'trapped' in the Union. This could be by the peacekeeping powers imposing sanctions in support of the peacekeepers on the ground (Table 1 in chapter 4, line 2). Or, with region B out of the Union the politics backing the peacekeepers could work to raise the rump Union's *post*-secession economic rents, for example, by increasing foreign aid, or, humanitarian assistance, or, opening up foreign markets to the Union.
4. Encourage the Union to look to the benefits of peace in a longer distant future than was the case when intense fighting had only just subsided, i.e., work to lengthen time the span over which political calculations are made (Table 1 in chapter 4, line 6). This could be brought about through assurances given by the peacekeepers and the wider international community that the Union will be welcomed and supported as a stable partner in the international economic and political systems.
5. Similarly, institute changes that encourage a Union to reduce its rate of time preference. If this happens, the leaders of a Union suffering short-term losses from secession, or, having to share power with a sub-national group, may find that the long-term gains from peace come to outweigh those short-term losses (Table 1 in chapter 4, line 4).
6. If a civil war was over sharing control of the multi-nation state, raise region B's expected economic rents while remaining in a reconstructed Union, e.g., through more power sharing at the Union level. That is, region B gains a louder political voice in the Union through which it can claim a better economic future (Table 1 in chapter 4, line 5).
7. If the war was one for secession, then raise the Union's economic rents with region B *out* of the Union—'it's ok to let B go'. This could be the case if the Union was persuaded by generous foreign aid and the opening of foreign commodity and financial markets to it (Table 1 in chapter 4, line 5).

5 UN Peacekeeping

UN peacekeeping operations are authorized by the 15 member Security Council and they are funded through a funding-formula agreed in the UN General Assembly where annual budgets are also voted on.[5] As failure to pay mandated contributions to the UN is not widespread free-riding is not a problem of significance—see Shimizu (2005). However, in the Security Council in March 2018 the US Ambassador said that the USA would unilaterally cut its long agreed share of the UN's peacekeeping budget from 28.5% to 25%—the following year there were shortfalls in UN peacekeeping budgets in several missions in Africa.[6]

Limits on funding and mis-design of some peacekeeping missions have led to a criticism that the UN does not achieve some objectives. Autesserre (2019) admits that: 'The ambition of their task is immense…U.N. peacekeepers are invited into war-torn countries and charged with maintaining peace and security. In most cases, that means nothing less than transforming states and societies. Peacekeepers set out to protect civilians, train police forces, disarm militias, monitor human rights abuses, organize elections, provide emergency relief, rebuild court systems, inspect prisons, and promote gender equality. And they attempt all of that in places where enduring chaos has defied easy solution; otherwise, they wouldn't be there to begin with' (Autesserre, p. 101). However, the 'endeavor has a spotty track record … U.N. peacekeepers too often fail to meet their most basic objectives. On many deployments, they end up watching helplessly while war rages. On others, they organize elections and declare victory, but without having fixed the root causes that brought them there—making it all too likely that fighting will flare again before long' (pp. 101–102).[7] And, while he admits that expert opinion

[5] UN, "Resolution adopted by the General Assembly" [*on the report of the Fifth Committee (A/55/712)*] 55/235. "Scale of assessments for the apportionment of the expenses of United Nations peacekeeping operations", 23 December, 2000. See also General Assembly of the United Nations, "Administrative and Budgetary"—Fifth Committee. http://www.un.org/en/ga/fifth/pkofinancing.shtml.

[6] See Peltz, J., "US Will Only Pay 25% of UN Peacekeeping from Now on Haley says", *Military Times*, March 19, 2018. And Wainer, D., "US and China Quietly AGREE on UN Cuts as they Feud Over Trade", *Bloomberg Business News,* June 27, 2019.

[7] Examples of what Autesserre, S. (2019) claims are UN peacekeeping failures are Somalia in 1993, Rwanda in 1994 Srebrenica in 1995, and in the Golan Heights at the end of the 1973 Yom Kippur War.

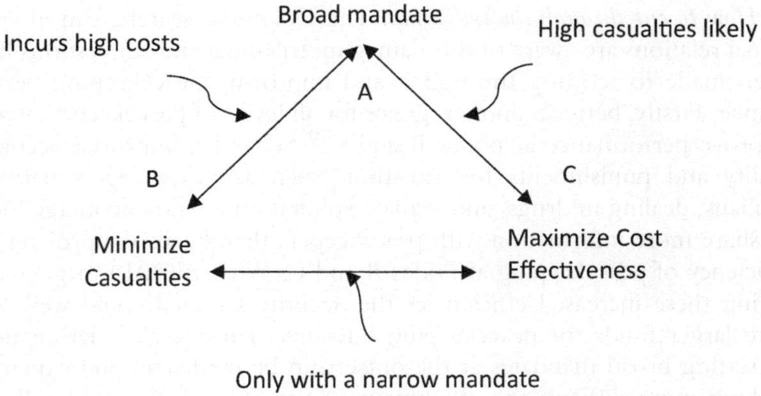

Fig. 2 UN peacekeeping trilemma (*Source* Author's creation)

is split on the issue of success or failure, he strongly leans to the side of 'failure'.

Mitigating circumstances are pointed to by Williams (2020), especially that UN peacekeeping missions face financial and other difficulties that stem from the multiple objectives set by the Security Council. These objectives are: (A) the adoption of a broad mandate to deal with the multiple issues that arise in peacekeeping missions; (B) minimization of casualties among peacekeepers; (C) maximization of cost effectiveness—i.e., 'keep the costs of peacekeeping down'.

Williams (2020) argues that all three objectives are difficult if not impossible to achieve at the same time—there is a 'trilemma' as shown in Fig. 2. Setting a broad mandate and the objective of minimizing casualties conflicts with the objective of keeping costs down (combining A—B conflicts with C); while setting a broad mandate and economizing on costs conflicts with minimizing casualties (combining A—C conflicts with B); and minimizing casualties combined with cost effectiveness likely means that a narrow mandate has to be set by the Security Council (combining B—C conflicts with A).[8]

[8] As Williams (2020) put it—'Specifically, Security Council resolutions oblige peacekeepers to implement broad mandates (often in high-threat environments), yet the Council designs missions to be much smaller than relevant military doctrine suggests in order to

How to cut through the trilemma: The UN and researchers in international relations are aware of this damaging trilemma and suggestions have been made for cutting through it and improving peacekeeping performance. Firstly, better training regimes for all levels of peacekeepers would improve performance at nodes B and C.[9] Secondly, improved accountability and punishments for violations such as peacekeepers harming civilians, dealing in drugs, and sexual exploitation would encourage locals to share more information with peacekeepers thereby also improving the efficiency of peacekeeping at nodes B and C. Whalan (2014) argues that seeing these increased efficiencies the Security Council could well then vote larger funds for peacekeeping missions. Thirdly, considering node A, setting broad mandates at the outset can be inefficient and expensive making more difficult the attainment of the objectives at nodes B and C. Encouragingly, UN (2015) recognizes that peacekeeping tasks should be set sequentially, thereby reducing task complexity. Only after gaining more knowledge of the on-the-ground situation should new (and better) focused tasks then be set.

A fourth reform recommended by Williams (2020) is that UN members should vote more money for peacekeeping which, in combination with the first three reforms, he argues, would pay for themselves because peacekeeping operations would likely become of shorter durations.

6 Other Peacekeeping Missions and Free Riding

Peacekeeping missions outside of the UN's orbit no doubt face similar 'design' problems but, in addition, they face the problem of free riding—whereby one or more 'interested parties' choose not to contribute so 'free riding' on the efforts of more committed countries.

There is a large literature on the public-private good characteristic of international peacekeeping—for example, see Bobrow and Boyer (1997),

save money. Furthermore, the Council prioritizes the safety and security of UN peacekeepers to avoid alienating the states that provide most of the field personnel' (p. 480). And 'The three competing pressures on the Council continue to affect all multidimensional UN missions because each one has to be generated from scratch from unpredictable and fluid partnerships between member states, the UN Secretariat and private contractors. Overall, the trilemma has constrained the design of peacekeeping operations and set them up for failure' (p. 480).

[9] In 2018, stepped up peacekeeping training was reported—see Peltz, ibid.

Seiglie (2005), Mendez (1999) and Shimizu and Sandler (2010). Khanna et al. (1998) emphasize that international peacekeeping is a mixed good with pure public good characteristics at one end of the spectrum and with increasing degrees of internalized benefits moving toward the pure private good end of the spectrum. Private good characteristics include maintaining good relations with allies, substituting low-cost peacekeeping expenditures for more expensive defense expenditures, gaining recognition in the international community for being a good world citizen that may then be 'traded' for other benefits, and limiting negative spillovers from internal conflicts in a nearby country. Regan (1998) discusses motivations of peacekeepers pointing to both realism (i.e., self-interest) and idealism (such as humanitarian motivations). Also, Chang and Sanders (2009) claim that intervention on behalf of an incumbent government may be self-interested—as when safeguarding existing trade relationships, natural resource supplies, improved national security, or, geopolitical advantages, but that ethical fulfillment has public good characteristics when a group of countries share common values.

There is empirical work supporting the free-riding hypothesis. Khanna et al. (1998) test the null hypothesis that if peacekeeping expenditures do not have a high degree of 'privateness' there should be no rank correlation between the ratio of the size of burden shouldered (measured by the ratio of peacekeeping expenditure to gdp) and the size of gdp. However, they reject this null in their 1990s data set for NATO members and for a wider group of countries finding statistically significant positive correlations. They take this as indicating that countries with higher gdps carry greater peacekeeping burdens substituting for countries that have chosen lesser burdens. That is, the higher is a country's gdp the greater is the proportionate burden it takes on, filling in for the lower proportionate burdens chosen by lower gdp countries. Closely related is the finding of Gonzalez and Montolio (2001) who use an econometric model to investigate whether Spain practiced free-riding on NATO defense spending after it had joined the alliance in 1982. They find that the level of Spain's defense spending, after taking account of control variables, is negatively associated with lagged NATO spending—which they take as evidence of free riding. Indeed, there is a significant literature on free-riding on other countries' national defense expenditures in alliances beginning with Olson and Zeckhauser (1966). Gates and Terasawa (2003) argue that the degree of free riding depends on the extent to which private benefits are gained from defense spending and this can change over time. The scope for free-riding under the nuclear umbrella offered by the USA in the 1960s they claim was reduced under the later doctrine of flexible response which offered more nearly private benefits which, if they wanted them, countries had to invest in themselves.

7 To Free Ride or not?

Discussed in this section are the economic characteristics required for peacekeeping agreements between countries to be self-enforcing in sense that a given country not only sees benefits for itself arising from a peace-keeping mission but that it will be willing to join that operation and, having joined, in the absence of unforeseen events, will not want to back out at a later date.[10] The key variables promoting self-enforcing contracts are:

1. Conflicts have negatively to affect potential peacekeepers, say, countries Y and Z, in some way—any of humanitarian, political, or economic concerns could be enough. However, if one or other country does not suffer any of these *'harms'* it will most likely not join a peacekeeping mission.
2. The *frequencies of conflicts* affecting the potential peacekeepers, countries Y and Z, have to be similar otherwise one or other will have no interest in joining a peacekeeping organization, say, with country K. If the frequencies are greatly dissimilar, the countries concerned effectively fall into different classes as to how often they perceive a need for peacekeeping operations.
3. *Harm-cost* of a conflict to potential peacekeepers must be more than inconsequential because if it is small, and given that peacekeepers incur costs, there is little incentive to intervene.
4. Similarly, with *intervention costs*, high values narrow the scope for peacekeeping.

[10] On the economics of self-enforcing contracts, see: Tesler (1980). A self-enforcing contract is one where signatories see themselves as being better off maintaining the contract than reneging on it. Self-enforcement is improved if all sides of a contract understand that if one signatory reneges all other signatories will also renege—which is known as the 'grim strategy'. If so, the choice for any given signatory is to enjoy the benefit of the agreement or to have no benefits at all.

5. *Reduction in the in probability, p, of a conflict* prolonging itself, $p_1 - p_2$, where p_2 is the lower probability after an extra peacekeeper has been added, should be large because this increasing the incentive for a new peacekeeper to join an alliance. By doing so, they expect to 'make a difference'.
6. Potential peacekeeper ***discount*** rates must not be too high, otherwise the present cost of investment in peacekeeping would not be justified by the (small) discounted value of expected future benefits. Impatience for success therefore must not be too great. Moreover, widely different discount rates can be responsible for some features of the structure of some peacekeeping missions. For example, countries with higher discount rates are likely to take on lower burdens—less expenditure or taking on only less risky administrative roles, than are countries will lower discount rates who value the benefits of peacekeeping into a more distant future. These latter countries may well spend more on peacekeeping and perform more risky activities such as sending troops.

8 Conclusions

Peacekeeping fits in well with the analytical approach of this book because the ***raison d'etra*** of peacekeeping missions is to move a country from a state of war ultimately to a peaceful secession, or, to a reconstituted stable 'Empire' were all sub-nation groups accept the benefits of living together, or, to a state of peace with a neighboring country. That is, peacekeeping is meant to interfere with unfettered historical sequences.

Peacekeeping though is not without its own problems—problems that can constrain the effectiveness of the peacekeepers. UN peacekeeping missions can be beset with design, funding, and manpower problems, but not serious problems of free riding; NATO and other non-UN missions do face the free riding problem.

The UN and researchers in international relations are aware that UN peacekeeping missions face design problems and reforms and suggestions for further reforms have been made for raising their efficacy, especially in the design stage at the Security Council level. As to peacekeeping missions that face free riding issues this chapter has pointed to what factors may make them better financed with reference to the literature on self-enforcing contracts.

In the meantime, all peacekeeping missions and their personnel should be applauded for the work they do often in very dangerous circumstances.

References

Autesserre, S. (2019, January–February). The Crisis of Peacekeeping. *Foreign Affairs, 98*(1), 101–116.

Bobrow, D. B., & Boyer, M. A. (1997). Maintaining System Stability: Contributions to Peacekeeping Operations. *The Journal of Conflict Resolution, 41*(6), 723–748.

Chang, Yang-Ming, & Sanders, S. (2009). Raising the Cost of Rebellion: The Role of Third-Party Intervention in Intrastate Conflict. *Defence and Peace Economics, 20*(3), 149–169.

Fortna, V. P. (2008). *Does Peacekeeping Work? Shaping Belligerents' Choices After Civil War*. Princeton: Princeton University Press.

Gates, W. R., & Terasawa, K. L. (2003). Reconsidering Publicness in Alliance Defense Expenditures: NATO Expansion and Burden Sharing. *Defence and Peace Economics, 14*(5), 369–383.

Gonzalez, P., & Montolio, D. (2001). Has Spain Been Free-Riding in NATO? An Econometric Approach. *Defence and Peace Economics, 12,* 465–485.

Howard, L. M. (2008). *UN Peacekeeping in Civil War*. Cambridge: Cambridge University Press.

Khanna, J., Sandler, T., & Shimizu, H. (1998). Sharing the Financial Burden for UN and NATO Peacekeeping, 1976–1996. *Journal of Conflict Resolution, 42*(2), 176–195.

Mendez, R. P. (1999). Peace as a Global Public Good. In I. Kaul, I. Grunberg & M. A. Stern (Eds.), *Global Public Goods,* published for the United Nations Development Program by Oxford University Press, Oxford.

Olson, M., & Zeckhauser, R. (1966). An Economic Theory of Alliances. *Review of Economics and Statistics, 48*(3), 266–279.

Regan, P. M. (1998). Choosing to Intervene: Outside Interventions into Internal Conflicts as a Policy Choice. *Journal of Politics, 60*(3), 754–779.

Seiglie, C. (2005). Efficient Peacekeeping for a New World Order. *Peace Economics, Peace Science and Public Policy, 11,* 2.

Shimizu, H. (2005). An Economic Analysis of the UN Peacekeeping Assessment System. *Defence and Peace Economics, 16*(1), 1–18.

Shimizu, H., & Sandler, T. (2010). Recent Peacekeeping Burden Sharing. *Applied Economics Letters, 17*(15), 1479–1484.

Tesler, L. G. (1980). A Theory of Self-enforcing Agreements. *Journal of Business, 53*(1), 27–44.

United Nations. (2015). *Report of the High-level Independent Panel on Peacekeeping Operations*, UN, New York, pp. viii, xi, 38, 48.

Visoka, G., Doyle, J., & Newman, E. (2020). *Routledge Handbook of State Recognition,* editors. New York: Routledge.

Whalan, J. (2014). *How Peace Operations Work: Power Legitimacy and Effectiveness*. Oxford: Oxford University Press.

Williams, P. D. (2020). The Security Constraints Peacekeeping Trilemma. *International Affairs, 96*(2), 479–499.

CHAPTER 7

Case Study: Secessionists Motives in the American Civil War

Abstract This chapter offers an empirical examination of the American civil war, 1861–1865, looking at the secessionist's side. The model developed in Chapter 2 is used to compare the benefits of retaining slave wealth (the rents) with the costs of the civil war fought to keep it (the dispute costs). Expected benefits are weighted by probabilities of victory and time preferences. It is shown that war costs might have been recovered in as little as six years. Also discussed is how the benefits of secession may quantitatively have been divided between the greed motive of retaining slave wealth and the grievance motive of states' rights.

Keywords Confederacy objectives · Slave wealth · States' rights · War costs · Willingness to pay for secession

1 Introduction

This chapter offers an application of the economic model of historical sequencing introduced in Chapters 2 and 3. The Confederate secessionist motives in the American civil war are examined—were they motivated to secede to protect slave wealth, or, was the main motive political, the protection of state's rights from interference by the Union, or, was it both in some combination?

P. Hallwood, *Interpreting Historical Sequences Using Economic Models*,
https://doi.org/10.1007/978-3-030-53854-5_7

Economic historians have established that the slave system in the USA was profitable but not hugely so with internal rates of return on plantation agriculture only a little greater than interest rates on railway bonds.[1] Maintenance of a threatened profitable enterprise is of itself not a cause for war; there is also the matter of expected war costs: Would enjoyment of the economic benefits of slavery in the future be enough to outweigh these costs? And if it was thought that they did, how quickly might war costs be expected to be paid back? Waiting, say, 6 years is one thing, waiting 25 years is of a different order of magnitude because the payoffs would be near or beyond the life-expectancies of many slave owners. It is also natural to assess the likely probabilities of victory in a war of secession and to weight the expected benefits of the continuation of the slave system with those probabilities. Quantification of these issues as they relate to the American civil war is the intent of this chapter, but they also relate to the broader literature on the causes of civil as discussed in Chapters 1–4.

An important question concerns what factors bind secessionist movements together? Several points stand out in the case of the American civil war: first, from the 1860 Census slavery was widespread in the Confederacy: in the lower south 36.7% of white families owned slaves; in the middle south 25.3% did.[2] The combined proportion for the Confederacy was 30.8% but it was much lower in southern states not seceding, being only 15.9%. Secondly, Wooster (1962) found a strong positive correlation within southern states between slave ownership at the county level and delegates voting for secession. Specifically, where slaves made up more than 62.5% of a county's population its delegates strongly favored voting for secession, while in counties with smaller slave populations this tendency was weaker. He concluded that delegates voting for secession did so because they saw it as the means of protecting the existing economic and social order based on slavery. Thirdly, as Abbott (1863) observed, there was a lot of intimidation in the south of slave owners who did not support secession by some of those that did. Fourthly, the US civil war bears out an observation of Collier and Hoeffler (2004) that 'opportunity' is an explanatory variable for civil war: the decentralized

[1] See Conrad and Meyer (1958, 1964), Evans (1962), Fogel and Engerman (1974), Govan (1942), and Gunderson (1974).

[2] Selected Statistics on Slavery in the United States, http://faculty.weber.edu/kmackay/selected_statistics_on_slavery_i.htm downloaded December 27, 2017.

governance system of the USA allowed factions disposed to secession to gain political power through the ballot box.

The four border slave states of Delaware, Kentucky, Maryland, and Missouri are not part of this chapter because they never declared secession. There was insufficient popular support for it with, in the Presidential election of 1860, John Bell, the non-secessionist Constitutional Union Party's candidate, winning all Electoral College votes in Kentucky, and only narrowly losing in Maryland (Ellison 1862, pp. 58–61). The predisposition of border states not to join the Confederacy is also indicated, according to McPherson (1984), by the fact that in each of these states, more of the male population volunteered to join the Union than the Confederate army, something that supports the contention of Harris (2011) that Lincoln had 'resilient support' in the Southern border states.

In explaining the causes of civil war, relative weights need to be placed on the possible causes. At the time of the outbreak of the American civil war statements by leading politicians inferred grievance or greed motives. According to Dew (2001): 'almost all historians recognize the central role that the institution of slavery and concept of state's rights played in fostering dis-unionist sentiment in the Deep South. There is simply no way to avoid these two factors, in part because the secessionist conventions [of December 1860 and early-1861][3] and Southern political leaders referred to them constantly in their effort to explain why their states were leaving the union' (p. 10). Abbott (1863) writing in 'real time' described the greed and grievance aspects clearly. With respect to greed: 'Shall there be in the USA an aristocratic class, maintained by the Constitution who are to enjoy exclusive privilege, living without labor upon the proceeds of the toil of others, while there is a defrauded class of laborers, excluded from education and doomed to perpetual poverty' (p. 24). And

[3] South Carolina's secessionist convention emphasized the slavery issue: 'Those [northern] States have assumed the right of deciding upon the propriety of our domestic institutions; and have denied the rights of property established in fifteen of the States and recognized by the Constitution; they have denounced as sinful the institution of slavery; they have permitted open establishment among them of societies, whose avowed object is to disturb the peace and to eloign [i.e., carry away] the property of the citizens of other States' (*Declaration of the Immediate Causes which Induce and Justify the Secession of South Carolina from the Federal Union. 24 December 1860*). And within days of the South Carolina convention and unanimous vote to leave the Union, Alabama, Florida, Georgia, Louisiana, Mississippi, and Texas 'passed similar acts of secession' (*OAH Magazine of History*, April 2011 p. 39).

on grievance: 'The one incessant cry has been "Abjure your democratic constitution, which favors equal rights for all men, and give us, in its place an aristocratic constitution which will secure the rights of a privileged class' (p. 25).

Greed and grievance is clearly reflected in the political speeches of the secessionists: Confederate president, Jefferson Davis, in his inaugural address, February, 1861, gave the sole reason for secession as the protection of state's rights, the grievance motive:

> The declared purpose of the compact of Union from which we have withdrawn was to establish justice, insure domestic tranquility, provide for the common defense, promote the general welfare, and secure the blessing of liberty to ourselves and our posterity; and when, in the judgment of the sovereign States now composing this Confederacy, it had been perverted from the purposes for which it was ordained, and had ceased to answer the ends for which it was established, a peaceful appeal to the ballot-box declared that so far as they were concerned, the government created by that compact should cease to exist. In this they merely asserted a right which the Declaration of Independence of 1776 had defined to be inalienable...

Only a few days later however, Confederacy Vice President Alexander H. Stephens said that secession would protect southern institutions, slavery included:

> The new [Confederate] constitution has put at rest, forever, all the agitating questions relating to our peculiar institution African slavery as it exists amongst us the proper status of the negro in our form of civilization. This was the immediate cause of the late rupture and present revolution.... (Corner Stone Speech, March 21st, 1861)

This chapter also contributes to a literature that assumes that insurrectionists are rational decision-makers comparing expected benefits and costs of military conflict. Besley and Persson (2009), Collier and Hoeffler (1998), Grossman (1991), Hechter (1992), Keen (1998), and Miguel et al. (2004) offer explicit optimization or econometric models that estimate the facilitators of civil war.[4] Studies emphasizing greed—secession is expected to raise income levels as the secessionists expropriate the returns

[4] Blattman and Miguel (2010) in their comprehensive literature review note that the case study—such as here—is a valid approach.

on, say, minerals, or, the case of the Confederacy in the American civil war, maintain them at levels consistent with the continuation of slavery—include those of Lichbach (1995), Popkin (1988), and Weinstein (2007). Studies emphasizing grievance include Scott (1976), Stewart (2008), and Wood (2003).

The evidence offered here is circumstantial on the Confederacy's motives for initiating a war of secession. Circumstantial evidence is the inference that some facts may rationally be deduced from some other fact or set of facts (Morsch 1991). A finding that war costs were low relative to maintaining the economic return on slavery draws the inference that greed was an important motive. It is true that 'we cannot observe motives' (Collier and Hoeffler 2004, p. 565), but this does not mean that intent cannot be inferred: just as with somebody caught in the act of breaking into a bank with safe-braking tools in hand may claim that they were doing it because of a grievance that the bank had left the lights on and that their actions had nothing to do with the greed motive of robbery. A reasonable jurist would probably conclude that the latter was the true motive.

The next section reprises the methodological approach discussed in Chapters 2 and 3 and is followed by a description of the rationale for the choice of parameter values needed to solve the maximization problem. Then, in the empirical section, several credible scenarios are assessed estimating how quickly war costs could have been paid back along with an assessment of how the 'perceived total burden of Union' could have been divided between the economic cost of losing the slave system and willingness to pay to assert state rights. The final section draws conclusions—the main one being that the economic motive of protecting income from slavery was probably strong. This is because, given the huge value of slave wealth, war costs could have been recovered in as little as 6 years. However, using a six-year demarcation is a value judgment; if somebody was to argue for a shorter payback period then, as argued below, weights can be given to the greed and grievance motives in combination.

2 Methodological Approach: A Secessionist's Maximization Problem

Writing before the American civil war, the military historian Carl von Clausewitz said that the choice of war is always based on expected costs and benefits (Rapoport 1971, p. 13). The expected *net* economic benefit at time t (which will be taken as late-1860 or early-1861 when the first declarations of secession were announced) for an 'average' non-slave Southern citizen of seceding from the Union is calculated as *per capita* income, i, with secession, so retaining the financial return on the investment in about 3.5 million slaves (US Census of 1860), less the level of *per capita* income assuming that 'asset' was eliminated. Notice that the expected costs and benefits are calculated on a per capita basis in this chapter. Thus,

$$E(net\ econ\ benefit) = \sum\nolimits_{t=1}^{T} \left[\frac{pr_t(i\ secession)_t}{(1+r)^t} - \frac{(1-pr_t)(i\ Union_t)}{(1+r)^t}\right] \tag{1}$$

where *E(net econ benefit)* is the expected net gain from secession which depends on the level of *per capita* income with secession, *i secession* (retaining the financial return on the investment in slaves) and the level of *per capita* income without that source of income, that is, *i Union*, as in fact was the case when the Confederacy lost the civil war. As both monetary sums are probabilistic, they have to be weighted by their respective probabilities; pr_t, is the subjective probability of secession—that is, the probability of the Confederacy winning the civil war, in any given year $t = 1 \ldots T$. The probability of not having seceded in year t is $(1-pr_t)$; and r is the measure of a representative decision-maker's rate of time preference, or, impatience for future income, as measured by the discount rate. A low discount rate favors secession because the present value of future income on the investment in slaves is more highly valued than with a high discount rate.

As secession was resisted by the Union, the Confederacy had to bear war costs (which are also measured as a percentage of annual Confederate states non-slave *per capita* income). The expected discounted present value of war cost is:

$$E(war\ cost) = \sum_{t=1}^{K} (1-pr_t)\left(\frac{(\$war\ cost)_t}{(1+r)^t}\right) \tag{2}$$

where $(1-pr_t)$ is again the subjective probability of not having gained sovereignty in any given year, t. War cost is incurred over the period $t = 1 \ldots K$. In year K, the war ends either with secession or with defeat—in the latter case remaining in the Union and losing the return on the investment in slaves.

Civil war cost has two components, direct and indirect (Goldin and Lewis 1975). Direct war cost is the cost of raising and provisioning the Confederate army. Indirect war cost is the cost of lost output, or consumption *per capita*, other than due to the shift of resources to the military caused, for example, by interference of the civil war with ordinary commerce, or, the destruction of capital stock due to military activities on Confederate soil.

The expected *net* present economic value to a Confederate secessionist of continuing to fight for secession is measured as the discounted net of war cost increase in *per capita* income with secession:

$$E(increase\,in\,income) = E(net\,econ\,benefit) - E(war\,cost) \tag{3}$$

As war cost is incurred early, and bearing in mind that income *per capita*, fell during the war, the *E(net increase in income)* in Eq. (3) in part depends on how long a secessionists 'looks into the future'. Here, 'the future' extends to 1917 when the US entered World War I.

If the economic return on slavery was insufficient, there must have been other war aims. The obvious choice is the political motivation to preserve state's rights—the grievance issue emphasized by Confederate President Davis. It is assumed, therefore, that preservation of the income from slavery—the greed motive, can be separated from the state's rights, or, grievance motive; that is, regardless of the maintenance of slavery, the Confederate states wished to secede from the Union because it was their state's rights to do so.

The perceived total burden of remaining in the Union becomes:

$$\begin{matrix} Perceived\,total \\ burden\,of\,Union \end{matrix} = \begin{matrix} Estimated\,lost \\ economic\,return\,on \\ slavery \end{matrix} + \begin{matrix} Willingness\,to\,pay\,to \\ assert\,state's\,rights \end{matrix} \tag{4}$$

The economic return on slave wealth is calculated from the available historical data. The willingness to pay (WTP) to assert state's rights (measured as the fraction of income per head that the Southern states would be willing to sacrifice to secede) is calculated as a residual. That is, if the estimated lost economic return on slavery was insufficient to explain taking on the burden of civil war, what would be the minimum willingness to pay for asserting state's rights? As will be shown, depending upon the exact scenario, the loss of income from slavery is large enough to pay off war costs in as little as 6–9 years. If any of these time frames are considered sufficiently short, there is no need to invoke willingness to pay to assert state's rights. However, if the acceptable payback period was less than, say, 6 years (again depending on scenario) it is necessary to add a sum for willingness to pay to assert those rights in which case both greed and grievance shared as war motivations.

3 Parameter Values

An assessment of the proximate causes of the American civil war requires realistic values to be placed on the return to the investment in slaves, expected war costs, and expected income levels during the war and in the years following, as well as the other variables in Eqs. (1) and (2).

It is assumed that the secessionists made the best guesses possible about the sizes of the relevant parameters. They probably would have realized that during the civil war, and for some years afterward, income or consumption *per capita* in the Confederacy would be lower due to economic disruption. They would also have been able to guess at the fiscal cost of war to the Confederate states. We don't know what these and other parameter values actually were; the best we can do is to assume that their best guesses were reasonably close to the historical values uncovered by historians; the secessionists were realists. Goldin (1973, p. 85) says that as the cost of the US civil war was greater than the cost of compensation to buy out the slaves, the war must have been fought on the basis of an under-estimation of war costs. However, this chapter argues that, even if expected war costs had been correctly approximated, the choice of war by the Confederacy was rational given the relatively short payback period of war costs.

It turns out that the conclusions don't change much within the range of known, or, reasonable parameter values—in particular, the discount rate, the range of estimated *per capita* incomes derived from slavery, and expected income growth in the long run. Moreover, the expected cost of war can be varied quite widely without affecting the conclusions; indeed, some of the main conclusions drawn are based on the highest estimate of *per capita* war cost that is currently accepted in the literature on the subject.

To solve Eq. (3), parameter values are required:

Choice of discount rate is based on empirical estimates in modern wage data of implicit discount rates in jobs involving significant death risk.

Moore and Viscusi (1988, 1990a, 1990b), Viscusi and Moore (1999), and Shanmugam (2006) put these discount rates in the ranges of 1–14%, 9.6–12.2%, and 7.6–9.7%. Here, we favor an 8.5% discount rate which is approximately in the middle of these ranges, but two higher rates are also used, 10% and 12.5%.

It is maintained that even though these estimates of death risk-aversion are based on peacetime data, they are relevant to military situations because: (i) workplace death of a breadwinner may have a similar impact on dependents as death on the battlefield; (ii) according to DeLeire and Levy (2004), in modern data, 'worker sorting' moves workers more tolerant of risk into more risky jobs; the counterpart in the Confederacy was that those that could afford to paid others—poorer and less well educated—to join the army (Noe 2010); and (iii) as Viscusi and Moore (1989) find, discount rates fall with education level. However, this said, raising the discount rate to 10 or 12.5% does make some differences to length of payback periods, typically increasing them by one or even two years in Table 1.

Probability of victory. Friedman (1976, p. 282) argued that numerical probabilities could be assigned to 'uncertain' events; and this view, according to Vind and Grodal (2003, p. 198), is probably now the majority view among economists. Thus, individuals make informed assessments of the probability of predefined outcomes. Indeed, as the American civil war was a one-off event, only subjective probabilities could have been assigned by the protagonists. What then should the subjective probability of a Confederate victory be in the early days of the American civil war? While this is difficult to assess, a probability of 50% is assumed, which is consistent with the calculations of Gunderson (1974, p. 929) and is higher than in the calculations made by and Mitchener, Oosterlinck, Weidenmier, and Haber (2015) who say that it was never much more than 40%.[5]

[5] Indeed, confidence in the longevity of the Confederacy was not high from the beginning. This is implied by Razaghian (2005) who examines Confederate war financing. If the probability of victory was high, Confederate bonds would have been quite easy to sell; however, 'the first financial legislation of Congress was the $15 million loan authorized on February 28, 1861 .... Subscriptions were invited on March 16 and within the first two days of the loan's opening $5 million had been subscribed. But as hostilities at Fort Sumter escalated, by mid-May $5 million was still untaken and the loan was not completed until October of that year' (p. 13). In other words, investors' confidence in the longevity of the Confederacy was far less than 'perfect'. Or, as Todd (2009) concluded from his

Table 1 War cost payback period scenarios, years

	Rate of economic growth no war: 1.5% Probability of victory 50%		
	Discount rates		
	8.5%	*10%*	*12.5%*
(A) *63.3% war cost and four estimated lost annual incomes per capita*			
Lost income per capita 32.3%	9	9	10
Lost income per capita 33.3%	9	9	10
Lost income per capita 36.5%	8	9	9
Lost income per capita 41.9%	8	8	9
(B) *31% war cost and four estimated lost annual incomes per capita*			
Lost income per capita 32.3%	7	7	7
Lost income per capita 33.3%	7	7	7
Lost income per capita 36.5%	6	6	7
Lost income per capita 41.9%	6	6	6

Source Author's creation
Note Payback periods are number of years for income from slave wealth needed to 'repay' war costs assuming Confederate victory. Income flows are discounted back to 1861 from 1917

Slave wealth. Table 2 lists the amount of Confederacy wealth tied up in slaves in 1860 as estimated by the market prices of slaves; all the estimates are large—as evidenced by the share of *per capita* income represented by the return on slaves listed in Table 3 lines 6a to 6d. The reason for variation in the estimates is that, as the records of slave prices are incomplete,

Table 2 Estimates of Confederacy slave wealth

Estimate 1	$3.51 billion	Source: Table 3
Estimate 2	$3.06 billion	Source: Ransom and Sutch (1988)
Estimate 3	$2.70 billion	Source: Goldin (1973)

Source Author's creation

analysis of Confederate finance, "From its inception the Confederacy was engaged in a stuggle for its existence" (Preface).

Table 3 Return on slaves as a percentage of Confederate income per head, 1860

Annual gross return on slave wealth		*Source*
(1a) 3.51 bn × 10%	\$351 million	Table 7.4
(1b) \$3.06 bn × 10%	\$306 million	Ransom and Sutch (1988)
(1c) \$2.70 bn × 10%	\$270 million	Goldin (1973)
Annual per capita monetary net return on slave wealth		
(2) Confederacy white population	5,582,222	US Census (1860)
(3a) Annual return on slaves	\$62.9	Line (1a)/Line (2)
(3b) Annual return on slaves	\$54.8	Line (1b)/Line (2)
(3c) Annual return on slaves	\$48.4	Line (1c)/line (2)
Contribution of return on slave wealth to per capita income		
(4) Confederacy white income per head	\$150	Fogel (1989)
(5) Confederacy total income	\$837,333,300	Line (2) times line (4)
(6a) Return on slaves as % white income per head	41.9%	Line (3a)/line (4)
(6b) *ditto*	36.5%	Line (3b)/line (4)
(6c) *ditto*	32.3%	Line (3c)/line (4)
(6d) Return on slaves as % non-slave income per head estimated by Stewart (2005)	33.3%	Stewart (2005) used a 7.51% rate of return on investment in slaves. At a 10% return, this is equal to 33.3% of southern per capita income

Source Author's creation

they have to be based on samples of slave auction prices at several different locations gathered by various historians. Table 4 combines several sources to provide Estimate 1 in Table 2.[6]

All three estimates of slave wealth are used in the calculation of annual *per capita* income derived from slave ownership.

Annual returns on slave wealth. Table 3 presents calculations of the proportionate contribution to income *per capita* of slave wealth using

[6]Kotlikoff (1979, p. 500) claims that Phillip's (1941) slave price estimates are overstated; indeed, they are peak prices from the year 1860. They are included in the calculations in Table 4 because Phillips is 'a classic' source of slave price data.

Table 4 Calculations of Confederate wealth tied up in slave ownership

Age group, yrs	*(1) % of slave population*[a]	*(2) Number of slaves,*[b] *000s*	*(3) Average price of age group as % of peak price*[c]	*(4) Average price age group: col 3 x $1,800*[d]	*(5) Total value of age group. Col (4) x col (2), millions*
0–14	44.8	1771	40	$720	$1275
15–19	11.4	451	72	$1296	$584
20–29	17.6	696	100	$1800	$1253
30–39	11.7	463	90	$1620	$750
40–49	7.1	281	65	$1170	$329
50 and +	7.5	297	15	$270	$80
Sum Column 5					$4.27 bn
Sum Col 5 × 0.85 (allowing for lower female prices)[e]					$3.95 bn
Confederacy slave wealth (holding 88.9% of all slaves)[f]					$3.51 bn

Source Author's creation
Note [a]Conrad and Meyer (1964, Table 14, p. 72); [b]Based on Evans (1962, Table 1, p. 186), estimate of total slave population in 1860 of 3,953,760; [c]Estimated from Fogel and Engerman (1974, main text, Figs. 15 and 16, p. 72); [d]'Peak price': price for prime field hands = $1800 in 1860 (Conrad and Meyer 1964, Table 17, p. 76; Phillips 1941, p. 177, for mid-Georgia and New Orleans); [e]To age 19—accounting for over 50% of the slave population—female prices were slightly greater than male prices. Thereafter, female prices fell below male prices by between 20 and 40% (Fogel and Engerman (main text) Fig. 19, p. 76). In fact, Evans (1962, Table 28, p. 225) calculates female/male price ratios in the order of 90% in the period 1858–1860; [f]Of the total US slave population in 1860 of 3.953,760 those living in the Confederacy amounted to 3,521,110, or, 88.9% of all US slaves

the three estimates of slave wealth in Table 2 as well as an estimate by Stewart (2005). Conrad and Meyer (1958) and Evans (1962, Table 21) estimate of rates of return on slaves in the upper South of 9.5–11.3% *per annum*, 1830–1860; and in the lower South of 10.3–18.5%. Table 4 uses a 10% rate of return which is on the low side, possibly understating the dependence of Confederate income on slave ownership. The supposition, of course, is that the end of slavery would eliminate slave wealth and the income flows it generated—lowering Confederate *per capita* income accordingly.

War costs. Estimates of Confederacy annual, 1861–1865, war costs are reported in Table 5. These range from 13.55% of Confederate annual *per capita* income to 63.3%. Goldin and Lewis (1975) is the most comprehensive source for estimated war costs. However, their estimates have been criticized for over-estimating them. They calculate the fall in

Table 5 Estimates of Confederacy annual average war costs as percentages of per capita income, 1861–1865

	Sources and method of calculation
(1) 13.55%	From Goldin and Lewis (1975), Table 12: per capita annual consumption fell at a compound rate of 13.55% from 1860 to 1865—from \$86.51 to \$43.92
(2) 30.2%	Annual fiscal cost ÷ Confederate non-slave GDP. Numerator: annual fiscal cost: \$252.8 m (from Goldin and Lewis 1975, Table 2, total of \$1,011,000 over four years). Denominator: Confederate non-slave GDP of \$837,333,300 (calculated as Confederate non-slave population (US Census Bureau) *x* Southern per capita income of \$150 (Fogel 1989 Table 1, p. 85)
(3) 35.1% + 13.55% = 48.65%	The 35.1% figure is calculated as the 4-year-averaged present value of consumption shortfall (Goldin and Lewis 1975, Table 12) over 1866–1879. 1879 chosen because Temin (1976) says that all negative civil war economic effects had ceased by then. Discount rate = 7.9%
(4) 17.5% + 13.55% = 31%	Following Temin (1976), if all civil war effects on per capita income ceased by 1879, Goldin and Lewis's (1975) estimates are over-estimates (because for them convergence did not happen until 1909). The present value of post-civil war costs on consumption is scaled down by one-half to 17.5%
(5) 42%	Calculation uses Goldin and Lewis (1974) 'reported direct' civil war cost to the South (Table 1, but excluding their unsupported fall in capital stock of \$1,405,648,000), divided by southern white population (5,582,222) to get per capita 'reported' cost. This is then divided by 4 to give annual per capita war cost and divided again by income per head of \$150
(6) 53.7%	As for line (5) but using Goldin and Lewis's (1975) "adjusted" civil war costs (but again excluding unknown capital destruction charges). Total 'adjusted' direct cost becomes \$1,798,659,000
(7) 63.3%	Gunderson (1974, p. 926) puts total war cost to the Confederacy at \$2.017 bn., or, \$380 *per capita*. Annualized this is \$95 for each of the war years. Assuming *per capita* annual non-slave income of \$150 yields the 63.3% *per capita* annual war cost

Source Author's creation

Southern *per capita* consumption relative to what it might have been had there been no civil war to 1909, calling it 'indirect cost'. Discounting back to 1861 at 6% *per annum*, this cost amounts to a huge $1042 per capita. However, Temin (1976) argues that any impact of the civil war on Southern consumption had ended by 1879 at the latest. This significantly reduces the discounted present value of civil war costs. Secondly, Goldin and Lewis (1975) are criticized for offering no explicit calculations or sources for their estimate of capital stock destruction in the South (Kim 1998). Thirdly, Goldin and Lewis's (1975) interpretation of why southern consumption *per capita* fell is widely rejected. Kim (1998) observes: 'Economic historians have advanced a variety of explanations for the decline in southern income *per capita*. Whereas Goldin and Lewis attribute the decline to the physical damage caused by the Civil War, most economic historians blame the decline on the fall of productivity in southern agriculture'. Economic historians identify several reasons for the fall in Southern agricultural labor productivity: Wright (1978, 1986) to the end of the world cotton boom and the isolation of the Southern labor market; Ransom and Sutch (1988) to the withdrawal of black labor and the deadening effect of monopolistic credit markets; and Fogel and Engerman (1988) to the loss of economies of scale with the end of gang labor. Moreover, Temin (1976) points out that Goldin and Lewis (1975) did not explain how the civil war led to lower consumption. Additionally, the reduction in the South's capital stock seems to have been over-estimated given that war damage could not have been so widespread given the huge geographic area covered by the South's main industry, agriculture.

The upshot of this discussion is that the largest civil war cost estimate in Table 5 is 63.3% of *per capita* income.

4 Empirical Results

Likely civil war benefit-cost scenarios are shown in Table 1 with the underlying assumptions set out in pairs of row and column headings. For example, with an 8.5% discount rate, in the first row of Part (A), the recorded war cost payoff period is 9 years which is calculated with the combination (in the row) of lost 63.3% of income *per capita* war cost for each of the four war years and 32.3% lost income *per capita* from slave wealth should the slave system be over-turned. Also, in the absence of war, the assumed annual rate of economic growth in the Confederacy is 1.5% *per annum* (approximately what it was before 1860).

Raising lost income from slave wealth to 41.9% (the highest estimate in Table 3 line 6a) but retaining all other assumptions reduces the payoff period to 8 years. Two other sets of scenarios are also examined in Table 1 Part (A) using 10 and 12.5% discount rates. In both cases, the length of payback period is increased by one or year two years.

Using the highest estimates of war costs as in Table 5 lengthens payback periods. Table 1 Part (B) uses a lower (but not the lowest) estimate of war costs, 31% of income per capita, as also shown in Table 5. The findings are now that in all 12 scenarios, payback periods fall to just 6 or 7 years.

If 6 years, or, any of the other estimated payback periods in Table 1 were thought to be short enough to justify fighting for secession, the economic motive is a sufficient explanation for the Confederate state's secession from the Union.[7,8] There is no need to invoke a willingness to pay to secure state's rights; that is, there is no need to quantify willingness to pay to correct grievances to get to what looks like quite short payoff periods.

Invoking willingness to pay to assert state's rights—the grievance motive. Supposing that desired payback periods were shorter than those calculated in Table 1, it becomes necessary to quantify willingness to pay to assert state's rights, as in Eq. (4). That is, how much were the secessionists willing to pay to settle grievances against the Union? This question is answered by choosing a lower desired payback period than those in Table 1 and adding a sum to 'lost income *per capita*' of remaining in the Union.

Thus, using the scenario in the first line of Part B of Table 1 at the 8.5% discount rate and reducing the 7-year payback period to 6 years requires 'lost *per capita* income' to rise to 34.5% from the 32.3% lost income from slavery. Here, the grievance motive is of minor importance as it accounts for only 6.4% of the 'perceived total burden of Union',

[7] Payback periods are number of years for income from slave wealth needed to 'repay' war costs assuming Confederate victory.

[8] Income flows are discounted back to 1861 from 1917.

i.e., (34.5–32.3)/34.5. However, the grievance burden's share of the 'perceived total burden of Union' can be increased. For example, again using the first row of Part B of Table 1 but at the 12.5% discount rate, to reduce that 7-year payback period to 6 years requires 'lost *per capita* income' to rise to 40.8% and the share of the grievance motive in the 'total burden of Union' becomes 20.8% (i.e., (40.8–32.3)/40.8). And as another example, still using a 6-year payback period, in the last row of Part A of Table 1, at the 10% discount rate, to reduce that 8-year payback period to 6-year payback period needs the 'perceived total burden of Union' to rise to 100% of income, and the grievance motive would account for 58%, (100–41.9)/100, of the 'perceived total burden of Union'.

5 Conclusions

This chapter is a case study in the causes of civil war, specifically the American civil war looking at the side of the eleven secessionist Confederate states. Using the economic model introduced in Chapters 2 and 3, as well as best estimates of parameter values from available data, what is offered is a comparison of the expected economic benefits of secession with the expected costs of the resulting war of secession. The main finding is that war costs could have been paid back in the form of retained income flows from slavery in 6 years. If 6 years is seen as being an acceptably short war, the greed hypothesis—that secession was aimed at protecting slave wealth is sufficient for the outbreak of the American civil war. However, it is also possible to argue that secessionists might have found a 6-year payback period as overly long, in which case willingness to pay to assert state's rights has to be admitted. It is quite likely therefore that both greed and grievance were motivating factors in the American civil war.

References

Abbott, J. S. C. (1863). *The History of the Civil War in America: Origin and Progress of the Rebellion*. New York: Henry Bill.

Besley, T., & Persson, T. (2009). *The Incidence of Civil War: Theory and Evidence*. London School of Economics, EOPP/2009/5.

Blattman, C., & Miguel, E. (2010). Civil War. *Journal of Economic Literature, 48*(1), 3–57.

Collier, P., & Hoeffler, A. (2004). Greed and Grievance in Civil War. *Oxford Economic Papers, 56*(4), 563–595.
Collier, P., & Hoeffler, A. (1998). On the Economic Causes of Civil War. *Oxford Economic Papers, 50,* 563–573.
Conrad, A., & Meyer, J. (1958). The Economics of Slavery in the Antebellum South. *Journal of Political Economy, 66,* 95–130.
Conrad, A. H., & Meyer, J. R. (1964). *The Economics of Slavery.* Chicago: Aldine Publishing Company.
DeLeire, T., & Levy, H. (2004). Worker Sorting and the Risk of Death on the Job. *Journal of Labor Economics, 22*(4), 925–953.
Dew, C. B. (2001). *Apostles of Disunion: Southern Secession Commissioners and the Causes of the Civil War.* Charlottesville: University of Virginia Press.
Ellison, T. (1862). *Slavery and Secession in America, Historical and Economical.* London: Sampson Low, Son and Company.
Evans, R. (1962). The Economics of Negro Slavery, 1830–1860. In National Bureau of Economic Research, *Aspects of Labor Economics*, Princeton University Press.
Fogel, R. (1989). *Without Consent or Contract*. New York: W.W. Norton.
Fogel, R. W. & Engerman, S. L. (1974). *Time on the Cross: The Economics of American Negro Slavery.* Boston: Little, Brown.
Fogel, R., & Engerman, S. (1988). Notes on the Explanation of the Growth of Southern per Capita Income, 1840–1860. In R. Fogel, R. Galantine, & R. Manning (Eds.), *Without Consent or Contract: Evidence and Methods* (pp. 278–282). New York: Norton.
Friedman, M. (1976). *Price Theory.* New Brunswick and London, reprinted by Aldine Transaction.
Goldin, C. D. (1973). The Economics of Emancipation. *Journal of Economic History, 33*(1), 66–85.
Goldin, C. D., & Lewis, S. L. (1975). The Economic Cost of the American Civil War: Estimates and Implications. *The Journal of Economic History, 35*(2), 299–326.
Govan, T. R. (1942). Was Plantation Slavery Profitable? *Journal of Southern History, 4,* 515–535.
Grossman, H. I. (1991). A General Equilibrium Model of Insurrection. *American Economic Review, 81,* 912–921.
Gunderson, G. (1974). The Origin of the American Civil War. *Journal of Economic History, 34*(4), 915–950.
Harris, W. C. (2011). *Lincoln and the Border States: Preserving the Union.* Lawrence: University of Press of Kansas.
Hechter, M. (1992). The Dynamics of Secession. *Acta Sociologica, 35,* 267–283.
Keen, D. (1998). *Greed and Grievance: Economic Agendas in Civil War*, Adelphi Paper, 319.

Kim, S. (1998). Economic Integration and Convergence: U.S. Regions, 1840–1987. *The Journal of Economic History, 58*(3), 659–683.

Kotlikoff, L. J. (1979). The Structure of Slave Prices in New Orleans, 1804–1862. *Economic Inquiry, 17*(4), 496–518.

Lichbach, M. I. (1995). *The Rebel's Dilemma*. Ann Arbor: University of Michigan Press.

McPherson, J. M. (1984). Ordeal by Fire: The Civil War and Reconstruction. *Science and Society, 48*(2), 234–236.

Miguel, E., Satyanath, S., & Sergenti, E. (2004). Economic Shocks and Civil Conict: An Instrumental Variables Approach. *Journal of Political Economy, 112*, 725–753.

Mitchener, K. J., Oosterlinck, K, Weidenmier, M. D., & Haber, S. (2015). Victory or Repudiation? Predicting Winners in Civil Wars using International Financial Markets. *Journal of Banking and Finance, 60*, 310–319.

Moore, M. J., & Viscusi, W. K. (1990a). Models for Discounting: Discount Rates for Long-Term Health Risk Using Labor Market Data. *Journal of Risk and Uncertainty, 3*, 381–401.

Moore, M. J., & Viscusi, W. K. (1990b). Discounting Environmental Health Risk: New Evidence and Policy Implications. *Journal of Environmental Economics and Management, 18*, S51–S62.

Moore, M. J., & Viscusi, W. K. (1988). The Quality Adjusted Value of Life. *Economic Inquiry, 26*(3), 365–385.

Morsch, J. (1991). The Problem of Motive in Hate Crimes: The Argument against Presumptions of Racial Motivation. *Journal of Criminal Law and Criminology, 82*(3), 659–689.

Noe, K. W. (2010). *Reluctant Rebels: The Confederates Who Joined the Army after 1861.* Chapel Hill: University of North Carolina Press.

Phillips, U. B. (1941). *Life and Labor in the Old South*. Boston: Little, Brown.

Popkin, S. L. (1988). Political Entrepreneurs and Peasant Movements in Vietnam. In M. Taylor (Ed.), *Rationality and Revolution, 9–62.* Cambridge and New York: Cambridge University Press.

Ransom, R. L., & Sutch, R. (1988). Capitalists without Capital: The Burden of Slavery and in Impact of Emancipation. *Agricultural History, 62*(3, Summer).

Rapoport, A. (1971). Introduction. In *On War*. Harmondsworth, England: Penguin Books.

Razaghian, R. (2005). Financing the Civil War: The Confederacy's Financial Strategy. *Yale International Center for Finance*, Working Paper No. 04–45.

Scott, J. C. (1976). *Moral Economy of the Peasant: Rebellion and Subsistence in Southeast Asia*. New Haven: Yale University Press.

Shanmugam, K. R. (2006). Rate of Time Preference and the Quantity Adjusted Value of Life in India. *Environment and Development Economics, 11*(5), 569–583.

Stewart. J. (2005). The Critical Role of African Americans in the Development of the Pre-Civil War US Economy. In C. A. Conrad, J. Whitehead, P. L. Mason & J. James Stewart (Eds.), *African Americans in the US Economy* (pp. 20–31). Oxford: Rowman and Littlefield Publishers Inc.

Stewart, F. (2008). Horizontal Inequalities and Conflict: An Introduction and Some Hypotheses. In F. Stewart (Ed.), *Horizontal Inequalities and Conflict: Understanding Group Violence in Multiethinic Societies*. New York: Palgrave MacMillan.

Temin, P. (1976). The Post-Bellum Recovery of the South and the Cost of the Civil War. *The Journal of Economic History, 36*(4), 898–907.

Todd, R. C. (2009). *Confederate Finance*. Athens: University of Georgia Press.

Vind, K., & Grodal, B. (2003). *Independence, Additivity, Uncertainty (Studies in Economic Theory)*. Berlin: Springer Verlag.

Viscusi, W. K., & Moore, M. J. (1989). Rates of Time Preference and Valuation of Life. *Journal of Pubic Economics, 38*(3), 297–317.

Weinstein, J. M. (2007). *Inside Rebellion: The Politics of Insurgent Violence*. Cambridge: Cambridge University Press.

Wright, G. (1978). *Political Economy of Cotton South*. New York: Norton.

Wright, G. (1986). *Old South New South*. New York: Basic Books.

Wood, E. J. (2003). *Insurgent Collective Action and Civil War in El Salvador*. Cambridge: Cambridge University Press.

Wooster, R. A. (1962). *The Secession Conventions of the South*. Princeton: Princeton University Press.

CHAPTER 8

Minimizing the Cost of Union: Fiscal Autonomy and the Case of Scotland

Abstract Propositions from the theory of fiscal federalism are used to argue for closer matching of taxes raised in Scotland and spending by the Holyrood government. Incentives would then be enhanced for Holyrood to provide public goods and services in quantities Scottish taxpayers are willing to pay for. Empirical evidence shows that this increase in vertical balance improves rates of regional and national economic growth. Two sequential games are used to show that whether Scotland chooses first or second in the public spending game with Westminster it still ends up with overly-generous funding. The argument is made that in fairness to taxpayers in the rest of the UK (increased horizontal balance) Scottish fiscal autonomy should be moved to.

Keywords Democracy as enough · Federal and unitary states · Financing Scottish government · Fiscal autonomy game · Leviathan hypothesis

1 Introduction

This chapter discusses the case of unions where one or more regions have a significant degree of governmental autonomy. Scotland in the UK exemplifies this. It is accepted that the creation of a subcentral government in a region of different peoples, the Scots in the UK, or the Catalans in Spain, is a possible means of stemming secessionist forces, thereby keeping

P. Hallwood, *Interpreting Historical Sequences Using Economic Models*,
https://doi.org/10.1007/978-3-030-53854-5_8

the Union together. This can be expensive however if a Union's central government tries to buy allegiance with excessively generous block grants to subcentral government(s). It can also be unfair to taxpayers elsewhere in the Union.

Empirical evidence shows that excessive financing by central governments of spending at lower levels of government adversely affects economic performance at either or both the regional and union levels. This is because block grants reduce incentives at the subcentral government level to spend public money in an efficient manner or to design efficient tax systems (Oates 2005, 1999).

This chapter concludes with discussion of a simple game theory model that shows that a central government committed to keeping a region that has some degree of secessionist intent within its borders will probably end up having to 'bribe' that region with excessively large block grants. To avoid this ongoing situation, it is argued that central government has to commit to only 'fair' block grants and allow the region to make its democratic choice between secession or remaining in the Union.

2 Federalism

Federalism in a form of government where different regions of a country, say, Connecticut in the USA, Quebec in Canada, and North Rhine-Westphalia in Germany, have the constitutional right to make certain laws that apply to their region—especially on regional-level income and sales taxes and many types of expenditures such as payments to local towns and financial support for disadvantaged people. Federal countries are found on five continents and include Australia, Belgium, Brazil, Canada, Germany, India, Malaysia, Mexico, Nigeria, Spain, South Africa, the USA, and the UAE and they contain about 40% of the world's population.[1]

Unitary states, where subcentral governments may have legislative powers, as do Scotland, Wales, and Northern Ireland in the UK, are also found on five continents.[2] Regional governments in unitary states operate under laws passed by the central government, and central governments

[1] Forum of Federations, The Global Network and Federations and Devolved Governance http://www.forumfed.org/countries/.

[2] Unitary states include Algeria, Bangladesh, China, Congo, Denmark, France, Guatemala, Haiti, Iceland, Indonesia, Italy, Japan, Kazakhstan, Kenya, Philippines, and Uganda.

retain the right to revoke those laws if they so choose—in a federal state, central government has no such right, a constitutional amendment would be necessary. However, despite this clear legal distinction, for purposes of economic analysis, the term 'federal' or 'federalism' will be applied to both legal constructs.

3 Democracy and Secessionist Forces

Kymlicka (2000) argues that federalism is a means of holding multi-nation states together where 'multi-nation' means that different groups with a country see themselves as being separate from the rest; the Scots in the UK, the Catalans in Spain and the Basques in both France and Spain are examples. In the case of the 'mature democracies', such as found in Western Europe, he argues that it is because of the very fact that they are mature democracies that these multi-nation states have to allow secessionists to express themselves—suppressing them would be anti-democratic. And it is because mature democracies accept that regional minorities can vote for secession that minorities do *not* vote for secession because they value the democracy of the multi-nation union they live in. Indeed, 'Nationalism has torn apart colonial empires and Communist dictatorships, and redefined boundaries all over the world. Yet democratic multi-nation federations have succeeded in taming the force of nationalism. Democratic federalism has domesticated and pacified nationalism, while respecting individual rights and freedoms. It is difficult to imagine any other political system that can make the same claim' (Kymlicka 2000, p. 213).

In mature democracies, therefore, 'federalism is enough' to promote national unity among different peoples. On this basis, as is argued below, there is no real need for central government (CG) financially to subsidize subcentral governments (SCGs) with the aim of 'keeping them in the Union'.

Both Quebec in Canada and Scotland in the UK provide test cases of the mature democracy hypothesis: the vote in 1995 on Quebec's possible secession from Canada was won by the 'remain' side by less than 4 percentage points. The case of Scotland in the UK is an ongoing test of the 'mature democracies promote harmony' hypothesis.

In 2014, the secessionist Scottish National Party (SNP) lost the vote on Scottish secession from the UK by ten percentage points which, at the time, was seen by many observers as being 'closer than expected'. In the

UK's referendum on membership of the European Union in June 2016 the UK voted by a narrow majority to leave the European Union. This offended public opinion in Scotland where the vote was 65% in favor of remaining in the European Union.

The ongoing test therefore is whether the median voter in Scotland values the British democracy of which it has been part of since the 1707 Act of Union, or, will it choose secession—a secession that would enable Scotland to rejoin the European Union if it so chose?

And there is also the matter of 'Its Scotland's Oil', claimed by the SNP with reference to North Sea oil. In a once secret government document, McCrone (1975) saw that North Sea oil tax revenues, at one time potentially huge in relation to public spending in Scotland, could promote the nationalist cause. He argued that to head off the possibility of secession, Scotland would need to be compensated through increased subsidies directed from central government in London toward it. In other words, if Scottish voters were not to move to support secession, Scotland required a *quid pro quo*. Scottish historians, however, have found no persistent Scottish secessionist threat. Miller (2005) wrote that 'arguably a British Government has implemented "devolution" [beginning in 1999] not so much because it fears Scottish nationalism and secessionism, as because it no longer fears them' (p. 8). And Finlay (2005) disputed the notion that separatism was an issue in Scotland for most of the twentieth century. It was only in the decades after the discovery of North Sea oil that secession had become a real issue, but even during these decades opinion polls almost always showed the nationalists with only minority support.[3] Moreover, calculations by the Scottish government show that Scotland has been in fiscal deficit—even including its geographic share of North Sea oil tax revenues for most of the twentieth, and after being briefly in surplus, in the period 2008–2020 Scottish budget deficits fluctuated in the range of 8–10% of Scottish gross domestic product.[4] Those are large budget deficits by international standards in high-income countries.

[3]Very many polls of Scottish opinion show support for the Scottish Nationalists fluctuating, but taking annual averages, typically over the last 34 years or so in the 23–29% range (see compilation at http://www.alba.org.uk/polls/pollwestminsteryearly.html). However, in monthly poll data support for the SNP sometimes approaches, or, even surpasses, 50%—for a compilation, see the Web site http://www.alba.org.uk/polls/pollwestminster74.html.

[4]Scottish Government, *Government Expenditure and Revenue in Scotland (GERS): 2018–2019*—see Table: Net Fiscal Balance: Scotland & UK 1998–1999 to 2018–2019.

Polling data suggests that for the last several decades Scotland has been unable to decide whether to remain in the Union, an impression reinforced by the fact that since 2007 the separatist SNP has formed minority governments in Scotland. Historians have suggested that greed drove Scotland to join the Union in 1707, largely for access to the markets of the British Empire, and did very well out of it. However, with the UK in relative economic decline, beginning in the early-twentieth century, Scotland has been encouraged to remain in the Union through allocations from Westminster of generous public funding. Indeed, as we model below, there is a game going on in which Westminster fears that unless it offers generous public funding Scotland will threaten to leave the Union. The advent of North Sea oil in the 1970s changed this game only detail—the flow of public funds to Scotland needing to be increased.

Stanley Baldwin, Prime Minister in the 1920s and again in the 1930s, said 'political unrest [in Scotland] was [not] in the interests of the Union'. He did not therefore seek to reduce allocations of public funds to Scotland under the Goshen formula (established in 1888) even though Scotland's population share had fallen below that used in the formula. According to McLean and McMillan (2002), the Goshen formula was used as the minimum share of UK public spending that Scotland would obtain through bargaining on a governmental department-by-department basis. Good bargainers could generally win more for Scotland. Things were little different in the period between Goshen and Barnett (1958–1978) when the Scottish Office bargained for public money on Scotland's behalf. Indeed, the Treasury's needs assessment exercise of 1979, using 1976–1977 data did find per capita public spending in Scotland (at 122% of England's level) to be above its needs level (estimated to be 116% of England's level). The Barnett formula was meant, over time, to bring convergence of Scottish public spending to the English level. But in over 40 years of the Barnett formula this has not happened. McLean and McMillan (2002) explain why: 'the reason for non-convergence [in per capita public spending between the regions] are political, not mechanical. Even the decision to persist with an incorrect population ratio was probably political. Scotland [in the 1990s] continued to pose a credible threat to the Union, which any SNP resurgence would bring back to life' (p. 10).

However, it is arguable that generous public funding is not necessarily an achievement for secessionist politics, rather, it has led to an overly large and inefficient Scottish public sector that has stunted Scottish private enterprise and it has not increased the rate of economic growth in Scotland. This is an example of the 'Dutch Disease' where the availability of windfall funds (in the Dutch case from North Sea gas) can stunt economic development elsewhere in the economy.

Immature democracies. It is in Eastern and Central European countries, described by Kymlinka (2000) as 'immature democracies', and in many countries in Africa and Asia which operate under less than democratic systems regional secessionists movements really can threaten secession: they want to express what they see as their rights to be free of countries dominated by people other than themselves. Countries falling into this category include Hungary, Kosovo, Moldavia, Poland, Romania, Russia, and Ukraine, and examples of these kinds of countries voting for secession include Bougainville from Papua New Guinea in 2019, South Sudan from Sudan in 2011, and Eretria from Ethiopia in 1993.

4 The Leviathan Hypothesis

Another potential advantage of granting a high degree of fiscal autonomy to SCGs, apart from possibly stilling secessionist sentiments, is that it can encourage efficiency in public spending such that economic growth in the region and the Union as a whole is promoted. The term 'fiscal autonomy' implies a high degree of balance between spending in a region and taxes raised there. In other words, fiscal autonomy implies a high degree of 'vertical balance' in the sense that relatively little revenue is passed 'downward' from CG to a SCG.

The Leviathan hypothesis is that when SCGs do not have to raise in taxes most of what they spend they will favor high levels of public spending and be relatively unconcerned about whether their spending promotes growth of the tax-base. Furthermore, regional voters are not in a position to constrain these tendencies because of 'rational ignorance'—gathering information on and analysis of government size and efficiency is time consuming and expensive, but any one voter has only one vote so that expenditure on 'discovery' of why government is so large and inefficient has low private return.

A solution to Leviathan government within a country is to 'make governments compete' with each other. This means that most spending and taxing should be devolved from CG to SCG—there should be a high degree of vertical balance in regional public spending.

There is a lot of empirical evidence validating the Leviathan hypothesis. Grossman (1989) argues that intergovernmental grants weaken fiscal discipline at the SCG level as well as encouraging growth of the public sector at that level. Mo Qiao et al. (2019) use a panel data of 76 developing and developed countries over the period 1972–2013. They find strong evidence that fiscal decentralization leads to smaller government sizes. Marlow (1988) argues that the 'inexorable growth' in the size of public sectors around the world is positively associated with fiscal decentralization.[5] In a panel of 32 developing and industrial countries over the period 1980–1994 Jing Jin and Jeng-fu Zou (2002) that increases in vertical imbalance between central and SCGs (vertical *im*balance measuring the difference between spending and tax revenues raised at the SCG level) increased the sizes of both SCGs and central governments. Similarly, Cassette and Paty (2010) in a panel of 15 European Union countries also found that greater vertical imbalance was associated with larger SCGs as well as central and combined government sizes. Likewise, Arnold and Blochlinger (2016) in a panel of 18 OECD countries found that moving the determination of tax revenue policy down to the level of SCG was associated with smaller public sectors taken as a whole. Accordingly, they supported the finding that greater vertical imbalance led to larger governments at both the SCG and CG levels. And Bartolini et al. (2016) using a data set of 30 OECD countries over the period 1995–2011 find that greater vertical balance between regional government spending and its own tax revenues provides an incentive for better use of resources, so promoting regional economic development. In particular, a 10% increase in vertical balance reduced regional income disparities by 11%.

The main conclusion is then that greater vertical balance in spending by subcentral governments—their spending being more closely matched with the taxes they raise at the SCG level—has economic benefits both at the regional and national levels.

[5] Anderson and van den Berg (1998), when taking account of non-market household economic activity in a sample of 45 countries, in fact find no relationship between centralization and size of government.

5 The Case of the UK: Reforming the Financing of the Scottish Government

By Act of the Westminster Parliament in 1998, the UK devolved many spending powers 'downward' from central government in Westminster to the new Scottish Parliament based at Holyrood in Edinburgh. At the same time, most spending by the Scottish Parliament was and remains covered by a block grant from Westminster. All the while the SNP has agitated for secession from the UK. In fact, reform of the financing of SCG spending in Scotland has been underway for some years, reforms that are inching their way toward fiscal autonomy for the Scottish Parliament—something that is also an intermediate aim of the SNP.

The 1998 Act granted Scotland limited power to vary UK income taxes levied in Scotland by plus/minus 3%, a power that was in fact never used. The Calman Commission's (2008) review of Scottish government finances said that it was not in favor of fiscal autonomy because it was 'inconsistent with the continuation of the UK' (para 6.31), emphasizing that the power of subsidization of Scottish government spending would be lost. However, it also recognized that the subsidy from CG in London meant that the Scottish Parliament had only limited accountability (para 6.26), and that increased vertical balance would improve accountability (para 6.30).[6]

The 2012 Scotland Act followed on from the Calman Commission and granted more tax power to Scotland, allowing it to vary its income taxes by 10 percentage points relative to UK rates. Two years later, the Smith Commission (2014) edged even closer toward fiscal autonomy for Scotland. It argued that the Scottish Parliament should have powers over setting tax rates and tax thresholds in Scotland (para 76), but the subsidy from central government should continue.[7] It was also recommended that the Scottish Parliament ought to have borrowing powers to finance any budget deficits in excess of its own taxes and the block grant from central

[6] Commission on Scottish Devolution, The Future of Scottish Devolution within the Union: A First Report, December 2008.

[7] Though it was recommended that it should be adjusted downward for the value of any taxes raised in Scotland that otherwise would have been raised by the UK government (para 95, 3, a), and upward for any spending transferred from central government to the Scottish parliament (para 95, 3, b).

government (para 95, 5).[8] Responding to the Smith Commission, the Scotland Act of 2016 devolved still more taxation powers to the Scottish Parliament now including some powers over tax rates and tax bands. However, the subsidy from Westminster was retained.

6 Taming the Leviathan: Fiscal Autonomy as a Game

It was suggested above that a move toward fiscal autonomy could raise efficiency in SCG spending, and it was also suggested that 'Scotland in the UK' is a test case of the 'mature democracy' hypothesis of Kymlicka (2000)—in multi-nation mature democratic Unions secession is not likely to happen because regions value the democracy of which they are a part. However, in Scotland's case, as of 2020, this hypothesis is being tested by the UK's decision to leave the European Union, something that was not supported in Scotland in the 2016 UK referendum on European Union membership. A Scottish secession referendum was held in 2014 with the 'no to secession' side winning. However, in a new referendum, Scottish voters will have to choose between remaining in the UK where they have a strong democratic voice in central government at Westminster, or, one day joining the European Union where Scotland's 'voice' would be far less loud.

To analyze the Scotland-UK relationship begin with the determination of the size of a block grant from a Union's CG to the a SCG.

6.1 Payoffs

The 'player' for SCG is the median voter in region B that is, Scotland. The CG player Westminster is assumed to have a preference to maintain the Union.

The SCG player can play one of two strategies: either stay in the Union (U), or 'threaten secession' (TS) by telling opinion pollsters that they will vote for secession. It is assumed that region B is poorer than the Union as a whole, or it has extra 'needs', perhaps because it has an older population that causes lower tax revenues (due to a larger share of retired people) or that more needs to be spent on them in terms of healthcare costs. A strict

[8] Report of the Smith Commission for further devolution of powers to the Scottish Parliament, November 2014.

'needs' assessment, NA, block grant from CG to the SCG would just cover these extra needs.

The Union also has two strategies: to make a 'needs' appropriation annual block funding allocation to the SCG, which is designated 'NA'. Or, the CG can make a 'large appropriation' (LA) that is larger than what is 'fair' on a needs basis. This large appropriation is made in the belief that it will stem secessionist desires on the part of region B's median voter.

Table 1 shows this game in simultaneous play, the payoffs are preference rankings for each player with 4 being the most preferred and 1 the least preferred. In each cell of the matrix, region B's payoff is written first and those of the Union second.

The Union's preference ranking from best to worst is:

- 4: U/NA—region B stays in the Union as well as receiving an allocation of public funds only in proportional to its needs;
- 3: U/LA—region B remains in the Union but receives a disproportionately large allocation of public funds;
- 2: TS/LA—region B threatens secession but is 'bought off' with a large apportionment of public funds;
- 1: TS/NA—region B threatens secession but receives only the smaller needs assessment transfers from CG.

That region B chooses 'stay in the union' is ranked as the Union's first and second preferences is reasonable on the assumption that the Union wants to maintain region B in the Union. That the Union ranks 'threaten

Table 1 Payoffs in the Union versus region B block grant game

		THE UNION	
		Needs Appropriation (NA)	*Large Appropriation (LA)*
REGION B	Stay in Union (U)	2, 4	4, 3
	Threaten secession (TS)	3, 1	2, 2

Source Author's creation

secession/large appropriation' above 'threaten secession'/'needs appropriation' is also reasonable but, as is argued below, is ill-advised, on the assumption that a threat of secession is more likely to lead to secession if region B was receiving only the smaller needs block grant.

Region B's payoffs are written first and the Union's second in each box. Higher numbers are preferred.

Region B's preference ranking from best to worst is:

- 4: U/LA—on the reasonable assumption that the median voter is not a committed 'nationalist', but wants to be compensated for remaining loyal to the Union. With this combination, tranquility rules in region B and in the Union—no threats are being made but the Union is paying for it with an overly large block grant.
- 3: TS/NA—region B's median voter threatens secession—tells opinion pollsters that he/she intends to vote Nationalist (or, actually votes Nationalist) if a larger compensatory block grant is not forthcoming. Perhaps he/she holds some sort of historical grievance against the Union.
- Equal third, scoring 2, are U/NA and TS/LA. The former of these is not welcomed by the median voter because no extra compensation for staying in the Union is forthcoming, only a needs block grant is being received, but the TS/LA combination is also not ranked highly because if secession actually occurred the large block grant would not be received and living standards would have to be adjusted downward. In fact, the outcome of the game in Figs. 1 and 2 does not depend on the median voter's ranking of U/NA relative to TS/LA. Instead of indifference, either could outrank the other without changing the equilibrium of the game.

Table 1 shows that if the game is played simultaneously neither player has a dominant pure strategy and that there is no Nash equilibrium in pure strategies.

In practice, the block grant game is played sequentially and roll back equilibria can be found. Begin with an actual case: the UK Treasury (playing for the Union) chooses its strategy first with region B, Scotland, choosing second. Figure 1 shows the game tree with the payoff rankings

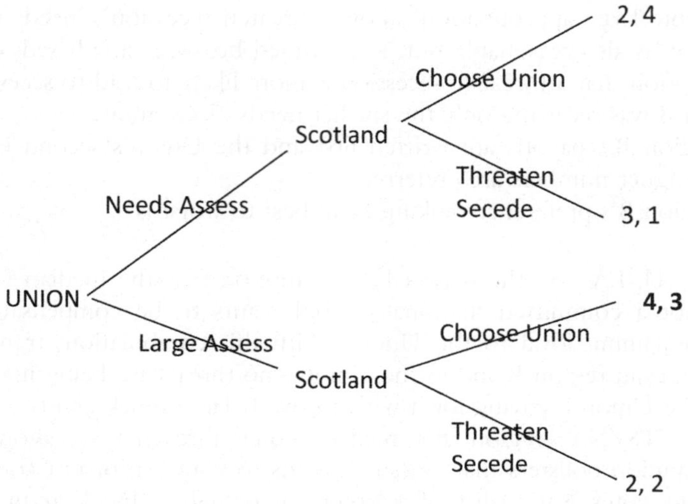

Fig. 1 Payoffs in the Scotland-Union block grant sequential game, Union chooses first (*Source* Author's creation)

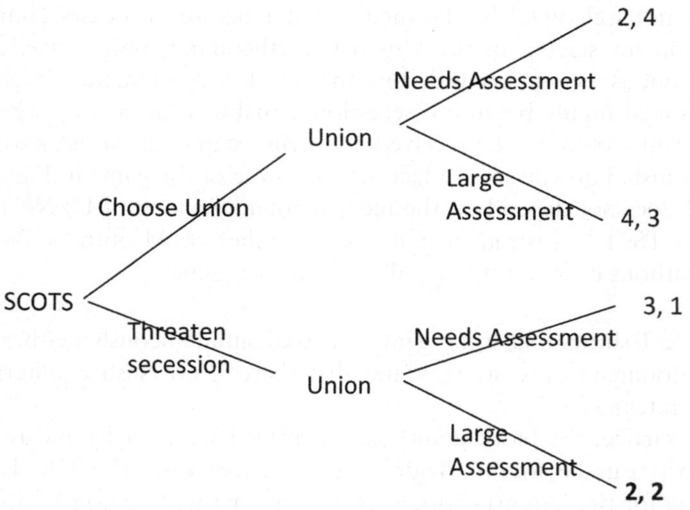

Fig. 2 Payoffs in the Scotland-Union block grant sequential game, Scotland chooses first (*Source* Author's creation)

of Scotland recorded as the first number. The Treasury reasons that if it chooses a needs-level block grant (NA), Scotland will choose threaten secession (TS) for a Union payoff of 1. However, if the Treasury chooses a large block grant (LA) Scotland will then choose stay in the Union (U) for a Union payoff of 3. The roll back equilibrium of this game is therefore U/LA with Scotland-Union payoffs of 4 and 3, respectively. Scotland stays in the Union.

Now suppose a sequential game in which Scotland chooses first. Figure 2 shows the game tree. In this game, if Scotland chooses U, the Union chooses NA for a Scotland payoff of 2. Should Scotland instead choose TS the Union chooses LA, also for a Scottish payoff of 2. Clearly, the Scottish median voter does better when it chooses second (as in Fig. 1, obtaining a payoff of 4)—which is the real-world case.

But notice that changing the play order only changes the game from 'harmony' to 'disharmony'. With CG choosing first (Fig. 1) there is harmony in the Union with the payoffs U/LA. However, with only a needs assessment block grant, which can be called 'fiscal autonomy', Scotland financing the rest of its spending by local taxes turns the game into one of disharmony because to get the large block grant assessment that it had when it chose second it has now to threaten secession (as in Fig. 2's lowest branch). Notice too that the equilibrium in Fig. 2 is [2, 2] while in Fig. 1 it was [4, 3], which means that changing play order has made both the Union and region B worse off.

An alternative approach is to change the SCG financing game to one of fiscal autonomy. Here, region B receives only the smaller needs assessment block grant and finances the rest of its own spending. What 'fiscal autonomy with a needs assessment' does in Fig. 2 is to cut out all the branches except the one at the very top which is Union/Needs Assessment. This branch is essentially the one that exists in the USA—each state chooses stay in the Union and CG chooses Needs Assessment with only limited transfers from the center to any given state.

However, there is risk for a Union such as the UK because losing its large assessment the median voter in region B may then vote for secession. However, if the Union stands firm, the median voter in region B would then have a choice between secession and losing the needs assessment transfers and independence. However, if the median voter in region B really does value the stable democracy of the Union of which it is a part, he/she would not vote for secession. But if they wanted to join some other democracy, a developing one still in its early stages—such as the EU, then the Union has to accept this—it would lose region B but save the money paid out on the large assessment.

7 Conclusions

Over the sweep of history, federalism has allowed minorities to flourish and choose not to press for secession. Unfortunately, many non-democratic countries, as well as in early-stage democratic countries such as found in Eastern and Central Europe, tend to suppress minorities and because of this lack of democracy, minorities sometimes press for secession to a much higher degree that they do in mature democracies.

However, federalism can lead to overly large governments at subcentral and central government levels. There is a large literature on this under the heading of the 'Leviathan hypothesis'. Thus, there is the combination that fiscal federalism—devolution of government spending to subcentral government—works in the political sense that it stems secessionist movements—at least in mature democracies, but that it can also prove to be expensive. The solution discussed in this chapter is that 'fiscal autonomy' can cut central government's fiscal costs of devolving spending to SCG. With fiscal autonomy, SCGs spend what they raise in taxes at their respective regional levels. This means that with fiscal autonomy there is much less vertical imbalance between spending and taxing at the regional level.

References

Anderson, J. E., & van den Berg, H. (1998). Fiscal Decentralization and Government Size: An International Test for Leviathan Accounting for Unmeasured Economic Activity. *International Tax and Public Finance, 5,* 171–186.

Arnold, F., & Blochlinger, H. (2016). *Regional GDP in OECD Countries; How Has Inequality Developed Over Time*. OECD, ECO/WKP(2016)53.

Calman Commission. (2008, December). *Commission on Scottish Devolution, the Future of Scottish Devolution within the Union: A First Report*.

Bartolini, D., Stossberg, S., & Hansjörg Blöchliger, H. (2016). *Fiscal Decentralization and Regional Disparities*, Economics Working Papers No. 1330, OECD, ECO/WKP(2016)54.

Cassette, A., & Paty, S. (2010). Fiscal Decentralization and the Size of Government: A European Country Empirical Analysis. *Public Choice, 143,* 173–189.

Finlay, R. J. (2005). *Scotland and the Monarchy in the Twentieth Century*, in Miller, op. cit., pp.17–34.

Grossman, P. J. (1989). Fiscal Decentralization and Government Size: An Extension. *Public Choice, 62*, 63–69.

JingJin and Heng-fu Zou. (2002). How Does Fiscal Decentralization Affect Aggregate, National, and Subnational Government Size? *Journal of Urban Economics, 52*(2), 270–293.

Kymlicka, W. (2000). Federalism and Secession: At Home and Abroad. *Canadian Journal of Law and Jurisprudence, 13*(2), 207–224.

Marlow, M. L. (1988). Fiscal Decentralization and Government Size. *Public Choice, 56*, 259269.

McCrone, G. (1975). *The Economics of Nationalism Reexamined*. Edinburgh: Scottish Planning Department.

McLean, I., & McMillan, A. (2002). *The Fiscal Crisis of the United Kingdom*, Nuffield College Working Papers in Politics, W10.

Miller, W. L. (Ed.). (2005). *Anglo Scottish Relations from 1900 to Devolution and Beyond*. Oxford: Oxford University Press.

Qiao, Mo, Ding, Siying, & Liu, Yongzheng. (2019). Fiscal Decentralization and Government Size: The Role of Democracy. *European Journal of Political Economy, 59*, 316–330.

Oates, W. E. (1999, September). An Essay on Fiscal Federalism. *Journal of Economic Literature, 37*, 1120–1149.

Oates, W. E. (2005, August). Toward a Second Generation Theory of Fiscal Federalism. *International Tax and Public Finance, 12*, 349–373.

Smith Commission. (2014, November). *Report of the Smith Commission for further devolution of powers to the Scottish Parliament*.

CHAPTER 9

Conclusions

Abstract Voltaire's Tartuffe got it wrong (as, of course, Voltaire knew): 'all is not for the best in the best of all possible worlds'. Over the ages, there have been so many contested secessions, so many empires, and so many interstate wars and, as many may say, 'not enough tranquility'. The people in the *Garden of Earthly Delights* (Hieronymus Bosch) would surely agree.

Keywords History · Secession · Tranquility · Turmoil · War

This book has considered disputes over borders as attempts to make (or, prevent) a 'transaction' in international law: namely, recognition of a new political entity, or the absorption of an existing independent entity into a Union such as an 'empire' like that of the Soviet Union, or the British Empire. Such a transaction incurs transaction costs, the costs of making a transaction happen, or the cost of preventing it from happening. Leaving transaction costs out is to miss the richness of historical dynamics. In the context of state formation or collapse, high transaction costs—defined in Chapter 2 as dispute costs and persuasion costs—tend to favor the status quo. If a potential secessionist has high dispute costs, it will tend to refrain from conflict and remain within the boundaries of the state that it is already a part. On the other hand, if the Union of which a sub-nation is a part has high persuasion costs it may choose to allow the sub-nation

P. Hallwood, *Interpreting Historical Sequences Using Economic Models*,
https://doi.org/10.1007/978-3-030-53854-5_9

to seceded, that is, to allow its own boundaries to shrink, especially if the sub-nation has low dispute costs. This balance of transaction costs is also relevant to interstate conflicts: high dispute costs on either side tend to favor harmony as no country wants to incur the costs of war. But low dispute costs on both sides can favor war, especially if the returns (the economic rents) won by the victor are thought at the outset to be high.

Altogether 12 historical sequences were discussed, nine of them in Chapters 3 and 4 relating to civil wars, secessions from existing states, and tranquility of sub-national peoples within an existing state. In Chapter 5, three more sequences were also described as they relate to the international context: as well as 'secure independence' there can be ongoing war, absorption of one country by another, and what was called 'harmony' when one country approaches another country to join together with it—as appears to be the ongoing case in the European Union.

These twelve historical sequences were uncovered using the theoretical modeling described in Chapter 2—modeling which is grounded in standard neoclassical economics where decision-makers attempt to maximize a utility function subject to a cost constraint. Potential secessionists look forward considering the likely gains from secession in relation to the expected costs of winning that secession. If the balance of these favors secession, then secession will be sort after, if not then a Union will remain stable—at least for the time being. A 'Union' could be an empire which, by definition, includes some involuntary members, or, one could be like the UK, four nations voluntarily together in a unitary state.

Several variables were identified as affecting the balance between the expected gains and expected costs of secession. These include expected economic rents within and outside a Union, the probability of achieving secession should it be pursued, the decision-makers' (the leadership's) rates of time preference, how many years the decision-makers look into the future (i.e., do they think only of the immediate future, or, to many decades in advance?) and the costs expected to be incurred in pressing for secession. These same six variables, most probably with different values, are also in the minds of a Union's political leadership and, depending on their balance, the Union may either accept or resist a secession by one or other of its regions.

Having established the decision-making model in Chapters 2 and 3 went on to discuss four potential political-historical interactions that can occur between a Union and one (it could be more) of its regions, which was called 'region B'. Tranquility reigns when neither the Union nor region B is concerned about secession (e.g., Scotland in the UK from the Act of Union in 1707 to the 1970s). A non-resisted secession occurs if region B wants to secede and the Union chooses not to resist (this could be the breakup of the Soviet Union in the 1990s, and it could be the UK if Scotland votes to secede sometime in the future). An 'empire' exists if a Union would resist secession but region B would not attempt secession because of the high expected costs of doing so (with a few exceptional years this could be India in the British Empire). Finally, a war of secession happens when both sides fight over the economic rents that an independent region would enjoy if it was successful in gaining independence. The history of the post-World War II era is littered with wars of secession as is recorded in Chapter 1 and illustrated in Chapters 3 and 4 where the emphasis was on discussing the causal factors as described in Chapter 2.

Chapter 5 went on to apply the decision-making methodology developed in Chapter 2 to *inter*state conflicts (or, the absence thereof). The four historical situations are now *country* B as an unchallenged independent country; 'harmony' (such as several eastern European countries seeking and eventually joining the European Union); war—as when country X tries to takeover country B but country B resists; and Empire, when country X takes over country B with little or resistance from country B.

Chapter 6 examined the role of peacekeeping in trying to end conflicts, both intrastate and interstate. Several episodes of peacekeeping were discussed, some of them successful—as with the UN's mission in South Sudan. One of the main topics of Chapter 6 was discussion of the financial constraints on peacekeeping. The financing of NATO is well known to suffer from a free rider problem, something that spills over into its peacekeeping missions. And, while the UN's financing formula rules out free riding because all members have to make their 'fair' contributions, financial constraints still remain a problem. The nature of these constraints and what has been suggested to do about them is also discussed in Chapter 6.

Chapter 7 looked at motives for secession through a case study—the American civil war. The broad history of that civil war was outlined with discussion of the Confederate voters support for it, as well as the mixed messages put out by Confederate leaders as to why secession was being pursued. Was secession about the protection of slave wealth or was it about 'states rights'. These two objectives fit in with the greed versus grievance conceptualizations of the causes of civil war. Using historical data, it is calculated that the costs of civil war to the Confederate states could have been paid back in about 6 years. The chapter then goes on to offer a means of quantifying the greed and grievance motivations lying behind this particular war of secession. It is suggested that this methodology can be applied to assess motivations lying behind other civil wars.

Chapter 8 offered a case study in a potential non-violent secession, that of Scotland from the UK. The chapter acknowledged that the UK, in the form of its Westminster government, has for many decades tried to stem discontent on the part of some Scots with large financial grants. These grants were and remain large given Scotland's relatively high *per capita* income in the context of the UK and, in only a few exceptional years, they have been well in excess of tax receipts generated in Scotland. Chapter 8 offered the view that to reduce the cost of buying off the Scottish secessionist threat, Westminster should devolve full fiscal autonomy to Scotland, meaning that spending by the Scottish government should be financed only by taxes raised in Scotland (but spending on things such as national defense and diplomatic services would remain the responsibility of the Westminster government).

As a final word, the complexity of the decision-making by secessionists and those that oppose them—as is shown by the twelve decision-related variables discussed in this book—underlines why it is so difficult to predict when and where secessionist movements will break out, or, even when existing movements will subside.

It is also clear that Voltaire's Candide got it wrong (as, of course, Voltaire knew): 'all is *not* for the best in the best of all possible worlds'. Over the ages, there have been so many contested secessions, so many empires, and so many interstate wars and, as many may say, 'not enough tranquility'. The people in Dali's *Premonition of Civil War* would surely agree.

Index

P. Hallwood, *Interpreting Historical Sequences Using Economic Models*,
https://doi.org/10.1007/978-3-030-53854-5

The manufacturer's authorised representative in the EU is Springer Nature Customer Service Centre GmbH, Europaplatz 3, 69115 Heidelberg, Germany. If you have any concerns regarding our products, please contact ProductSafety@springernature.com

Printed and bound by CPI Group (UK) Ltd, Croydon, CR0 4YY
30/09/2026
02225466-0010